JOHN

MESSAGES OF HOPE, FORGIVENESS, AND PURPOSE

John

Messages of Hope, Forgiveness, and Purpose

F. Wayne Mac Leod

Authentic
MEDIA

00 09 08 07 06 05 04   7 6 5 4 3 2 1
Published by Authentic Media
129 Mobilization Drive, Waynesboro, GA 30830 USA authenticusa@stl.org
and 9 Holdom Avenue, Bletchley, Milton Keynes, Bucks, MK1 1QR, UK

ISBN: 1-932805-00-1

Cover design: Paul Lewis

Contents

Preface

The Apostle John was the disciple whom Jesus loved. His gospel makes it clear that he dearly loved his Lord as well. John had a very high opinion of Jesus. He told his readers that his reason for writing this gospel was that they might believe Jesus was the Son of God and by believing, they would have life in his name. John carefully selected events from the life of Christ with this purpose in mind. No one can seriously read this gospel without coming to the same conclusion as John: Jesus is indeed the Christ.

It is my desire that the readers of this devotional guide see the Lord Jesus as John saw him. This is what John would have wanted us to see. If you do not know the Lord Jesus, maybe you will meet him on the pages of John's Gospel. If you do know him, my prayer is that this commentary will enable you to know him better.

I would encourage you to take your time reading this book. Read one meditation a day. Read the Scripture passage associated with each chapter. Pray over each meditation. Ask the Lord to help you see what he would have you see. Commit yourself to obey what the Lord reveals to you from his Word. I pray that this book will help the Gospel of John come alive for you and that it would have an impact on your walk with the Lord Jesus and your ministry for him.

My prayers go especially to pastors and Christian workers in Africa and Asia who will receive this commentary, thanks to the generous gifts of believers in North America. May you be blessed personally as you read. And may you know the rich blessing of God as you advance his kingdom in the midst of trial and difficulty.

Your brother in Christ, laboring with you for the sake of Christ,

F. Wayne Mac Leod

1

The Word

Read John 1:1–5, 9–14

Before he does anything else, John lets his readers know exactly what his purposes are in writing. This gospel is about the Lord Jesus Christ. In John's day there were many opinions circulating about our Lord. Some people accepted him as the Son of God. Others rejected him as an impostor. John writes so that all may know the true identity of the Lord Jesus. In the opening verses of his book, he tells us what he personally believes about his Lord and gives us a summary statement of his entire book.

In these opening verses, the apostle introduces us to the Word. Who is the Word? A quick examination of what John teaches us about the Word will remove any doubt in our minds concerning the identity of this person. The Word is none other than our Lord Jesus Christ. A "word" is the expression of the mind and heart. The expression of the mind and heart of God was given personality in Jesus

Christ. Let us examine what the apostle John tells us about the expression of the heart and mind of God as revealed in his Son, the Lord Jesus.

Jesus was in the beginning

"In the beginning was the Word," begins John. The Lord Jesus Christ existed when nothing else existed. He was there even before the world began. He had no beginning. As human beings we find it difficult to understand how something could have no beginning. Unlike us, the Lord Jesus always existed. It is true that he came to this earth in the form of a man. He lived among us and died on the cross. John is telling us here, however, that the Lord Jesus existed even before he came to this earth as a little baby in a manger. He existed before the world was formed.

Jesus is God

John tells us that the Lord Jesus was with God from the beginning. Notice also that he clearly tells us that he was God. There was no doubt in the mind of John as to the deity of the Lord Jesus. This was a belief that was widely debated in the days of John. There is no doubt here as to where John stood on this issue. Notice that John spoke of Jesus as separate from God and yet completely one with God. He was with God yet he was God. From this we understand that while the Lord Jesus has his own identity as the Son of God, he is still one with God.

Without Jesus nothing would exist

John reminds us that all things were made through Jesus, the Word (verse 3). All creation owes its existence to the Lord Jesus Christ. We do not usually attribute the creation of the world to the Lord Jesus. The normal tendency is to see God the Father as the creator of the world. John is telling us here is that the Lord Jesus was absolutely one with the Father in the creation of the world.

In Jesus there is life

John goes on to tell us that in Jesus there was life (verse 4). We have already seen that we owe our physical existence to the Lord Jesus who was one with the Father in creation. This is only part of the life that Jesus offers us, however. He also offers us spiritual life. You can have all this world offers and still be empty and barren inside. Jesus is also the source of spiritual life. Through his work for us on the cross, the Lord Jesus offers us new life. He comes to put his Holy Spirit in us, enabling us to enter a personal relationship with God. Without this life we would be lost in our sin and separated forever from God and his blessing. Jesus came to offer us new spiritual life. In him alone we can know this life in abundance.

Jesus offers his light to mankind

The life Jesus offers is compared to a light (verse 4). Without the life of Christ in us we are left in the darkness of our sins. We would not understand that we were without God and condemned to an eternity of darkness. When Jesus gives his life to us, we gain new understanding. His Holy Spirit opens our eyes to the reality of spiritual matters. This life he offers is an eternal life. It is a life of forgiveness and peace with God. His life in us radically transforms us in every way. We are no longer the same. We become more and more like the Lord Jesus.

Man rejected the light of Jesus

The sad thing about this light is that though the Lord Jesus shone in the darkness, the world turned its back on him (verse 5). As a child, I remember turning over rocks and watching the insects run for cover. They seemed to like living in the darkness. The light disturbed them. This is the image John paints for us here. Christ came and shone his light on us and we ran like those insects for the shelter of the darkness. Even today men and women are running from that light. They are unaware of the vastness and beauty of life in the light of Christ.

The Lord Jesus came personally to this world and lived among people (verse 10). The world did not recognize him. People did not accept him or place their confidence in him. Every breath they breathed, every beat of their hearts was a reminder of how much they depended on the Lord Jesus, their creator, yet they could not find it in their hearts to trust in him. His own people did not receive him. He came as a Jew. He was raised as a Jew. The people of his own hometown, his brothers and sisters, did not believe in him.

Although most of his own people rejected him, there were others who did receive him and believed in his name (verse 12). To these individuals he gave the right to become the children of God. Notice that becoming a child of God is a right that is given only to those who receive and believe in the Lord Jesus Christ. Not everyone is a child of God. We do not become a child of God by being born into this world. We must become a child of God by receiving and believing in the Lord Jesus Christ. Verse 13 tells us that becoming God's child has nothing to do with esh and blood. It has nothing to do with the decision of a husband and wife to have a child. The apostle John tells us here that there is a physical birth, by which we enter this world. There is also a spiritual birth, by which we enter the kingdom of heaven. We can experience this new birth by receiving and believing in Jesus, the Word. This is all there is to becoming a child of God and receiving the new life Jesus came to offer. Believe that Jesus is who he says he is and receive the life and forgiveness he offers to you, and you will be born again into this new life.

John concluded this section by stating that the Lord Jesus took on the form of a man (verse 14). He lived among us. Those who saw him saw the glory of God. He came from the Father. He was full of grace and truth. Grace is the unmerited favor of God toward a sinner. The Lord Jesus is full of grace. He wants to forgive our sins. He wants to draw us to his side. He wants us to know and experience the light of God. Notice also that Jesus is full of truth. This means that we can put our complete confidence in him. He is completely trustworthy. He will never fail. What he says will come to pass.

There is no doubt in the mind of John as to the identity of the Lord Jesus. He is God, the creator and sustainer of life. He is our hope of eternal life. He offers this eternal life today. He is full of grace and truth. Not only does he want to forgive but we can trust him fully to accomplish all he said he would. He alone is worthy of our confidence.

For Consideration:

• What are the conflicting ideas about Jesus in our day?

• What does John teach us here about the Lord Jesus?

• Why did the Lord Jesus come to this earth?

• Are you a child of God today? How can you know this?

For Prayer:

• Thank the Lord for coming to earth to reveal the light of God to us.

• Thank the Lord for his forgiveness and the spiritual life he came to offer.

- Do you have friends or loved ones who have not yet accepted this life Christ came to offer? Take a moment to pray for them.

2

A Man Sent from God

Read John 1:6–8, 15–34

We have already met the Lord Jesus Christ. John now wants to introduce us to the man called of God to introduce our Lord to the world. His name is John the Baptist. He is not to be confused with the author of this book.

John the Baptist was sent by God to be a witness to the light (verse 6). Verse 5 tells us that Jesus was the light that shone in the darkness. We are told that John the Baptist bore witness so that men and women would believe in the Lord Jesus (verse 7). It would be through the testimony of John the Baptist that men and women would come to a saving knowledge of the Lord Jesus. We too have been called to be a witness to the light. We cannot sit back. Like John the Baptist, we are the instruments through which men and women will come to know the Lord Jesus.

The apostle John wanted to make it clear that John the Baptist was not the light (verse 8). There were times when the Jews wondered if he was the Messiah. John the Baptist was careful not to take the glory away from the Lord. He was aware of his role as a simple and unworthy witness. He did not hesitate to speak of the greatness of the Lord Jesus. He told those who came to him that he was not even worthy to untie the Lord's sandals (verse 27). John the Baptist knew who he was. He was a simple sinner whom Jesus had touched and forgiven. He was nothing special in himself. His purpose in life was to point others to the Lord Jesus.

Not everyone understood the ministry of John the Baptist. On one occasion the Jews sent priests and Levites to question him about his ministry and message. They asked him who he was. There were opinions circulating in the community that he might be the Christ or a prophet. Some even believed that he was Elijah who had come back from the dead (verse 21). John was clear about who he was. He was a simple voice crying out in the wilderness, preparing the way for the Lord. He saw himself as being the fulfillment of Isaiah's prophecy:

> A voice of one calling:
> "In the desert prepare
>   the way for the LORD;
> make straight in the wilderness
>   a highway for our God.
> Every valley shall be raised up,
>   every mountain and hill made low;
> the rough ground shall become level,
>   the rugged places a plain.
> And the glory of the LORD will be revealed,
>   and all mankind together will see it.
>   For the mouth of the LORD has spoken."
>   (Isaiah 40:3–5)

Isaiah prophesied of a time when the glory of the Lord would be revealed on this earth. Before that glory was revealed, however, a voice from the wilderness would cry out to announce his coming. John was that voice. He understood his place and calling. He understood that he was the fulfillment of this prophecy. His calling was to announce the coming of the glory of the Lord. That glory was to be found in the presence of the Lord Jesus himself on this earth.

The Pharisees questioned John about why he baptized if he was not the Messiah (verses 24–25). Baptism was seen as an initiation into a certain faith. The Pharisees interpreted what John was doing as gathering disciples for himself. The understanding was that those who were baptized became followers of the one who baptized them. In verse 31 John the Baptist told the Pharisees that he baptized so that Jesus Christ would be revealed to Israel. He did not baptize to gain followers for himself but to point people to the work the Lord Jesus would do. We will examine the baptism of John the Baptist in more detail in another passage. Notice in the following verses what John told Israel about the Lord Jesus.

He surpasses me (verse 15)

We have already seen how John the Baptist told the Jews that Jesus was greater than he was. John the Baptist recognized Jesus as God. Jesus surpassed John, according to verse 15, because Jesus "was before" John. That is to say, Jesus existed from the beginning. John saw himself as a humble servant of Jesus, the eternal God.

From the fullness of his grace we receive blessing (verse 16)

John the Baptist reminded his listeners that they had received one blessing after another from Jesus. As the creator of the world, the Lord Jesus had blessed them in abundance. There is nothing we have that does not come from his hand.

Not only are we physically blessed by the Lord Jesus, but we have also received many spiritual blessings from his hand as well. What a wonderful Lord we have. How we need to bow down in thanksgiving to him for all that he has done for us. We have received from him one blessing after another.

He is the source of grace and truth (verse 17)

In verse 17 the apostle John reminded his listeners that while the law was good it could never save their souls. It only proved to them that they were sinners in need of constant cleansing. In the Lord Jesus, however, people received grace. He came to offer us complete pardon and cleansing once for all. He came to usher us directly into the presence of God. He came to give us acceptance with God. He came to forgive us from our sins past, present, and future. He is the source of abundant grace.

Not only is Jesus the source of grace, he is also the source of truth. There is much debate in our day over truth. There are many opinions about God and how we can get to heaven. While opinions vary, there is only one source for truth. Jesus is that source. If you want to know truth, you must come to Jesus. We dare not listen to anyone else. Jesus alone is the source of all truth.

He is the Lamb of God (verse 29)

According to John the Baptist, Jesus was "the Lamb of God, who takes away the sin of the world!" (verse 29). In the Old Testament, lambs were sacrificed for the sins of God's people. Jesus became the sacrifice for our sins. He was a perfect sacrifice. His sacrifice was a once-for-all sacrifice. He died once and paid for all the sins we will ever commit. There is no more need of a sacrifice for sin. Our Lord Jesus, as the sacrificial lamb, paid the price in full. Only through his work can we be forgiven.

He is the Son of God (verses 32–34)

John the Baptist declared Jesus as the chosen one of God. John saw the Spirit of God fall on him. The Lord had given this to John as a sign: "The one on whom you see the Spirit descend is he who will baptize with the Holy Spirit" (verse 33). John saw the Spirit of God come on our Lord in fulfillment of this word. There was no doubt in his mind that Jesus was the Son of God.

John baptized those who came to him to point them to the one who would baptize them with the Holy Spirit. His baptism was a foreshadowing of what was to come. He baptized people in anticipation of the Messiah's reign. An individual baptized by John's baptism turned his back on sin and submitted himself to the coming reign of the Messiah.

How about you? Have you submitted yourself to the reign of the Lord Jesus Christ? Have you recognized him as Lord of all? Have you fallen at his feet and surrendered to his lordship? Is your life wholly and completely devoted to the Lord Jesus?

For Consideration:

- The desire of John the Baptist here was that the Lord Jesus receive all the glory. Is this your heart's desire?

- What does John the Baptist teach us here about the Lord Jesus?

- John the Baptist was fully aware of his calling as a servant of God. What is God's call on your life?

- What is it about John's relationship with the Lord that you admire?

For Prayer:

• Ask God to give you a greater understanding of the ministry and person of the Lord Jesus.

• Ask him to help you to understand the ministry he has given you personally.

• Ask the Lord to give you a heart like John's—full of devotion and love for the Lord Jesus.

3

Jesus' First Disciples

Read John 1:35–51

n the last meditation we discovered that John the Baptist was called to testify to the Light so that all might believe. He was an instrument in God's hands for the spread of the good news about the Lord Jesus Christ. God would draw men and women to himself through John the Baptist. In this section we see that John was not the only one to be called to such a ministry.

On one occasion, as John was speaking to his followers, he saw the Lord Jesus passing by. "Look," he said, "the Lamb of God" (verse 35). When John's disciples heard him say this, they left his side and followed Jesus. Have you ever had someone leave your church to go to another? What was your response? Often, when this happens, there is a spirit of jealousy and bitterness. How did John feel when his disciples left him to follow the Lord? Later some of John the Baptist's disciples noticed that people were leaving their group to follow Jesus. They brought this issue to John's attention.

John responded, "He must increase, but I must decrease" (3:30 KJV). John was not in the least concerned that he was losing followers to the Lord Jesus. Here in chapter 1, John pointed his disciples to Jesus and watched them leave. He rejoiced that they followed the Lord. John was not interested in competing with his Lord. He wanted Jesus to receive all the attention and focus.

When two of John's disciples met the Lord, they asked him where he lived. It may be that they wanted to spend time with him and listen to his teaching. No doubt they had many questions that even John could not answer. Their former master had told them that this man, Jesus, was the Messiah, but they had to discover this for themselves. They wanted to sit down and listen to what Jesus had to say. They needed to see for themselves.

Jesus invited them to stay with him. The Bible tells us that they spent the day with Jesus. From verse 39 we understand that it was about the tenth hour of the day when they went with Jesus. The tenth hour of the day would be about four o'clock in the afternoon. We can only imagine the type of questions that these men had for the Lord.

While we do not know the subject of the conversation, we do know the result. Verse 40 tells us that one of the disciples was a man by the name of Andrew. The first thing Andrew did was to go and tell his brother Simon that they had found the Messiah. Obviously, Andrew's opinion was no longer based on what John the Baptist had told him. Andrew had now formed his own opinion about the Lord Jesus. You can sense a certain excitement in this verse: "We have found the Messiah," said Andrew. There is no doubt in his mind. He does not say, "I think we have found the Messiah" or "Simon, come and meet this man. I was wondering if he could possibly be the Messiah." Andrew's mind was made up. There was no question about the identity of Jesus.

John the Baptist pointed Andrew to the Lord. Andrew in

turn pointed Simon to the Lord. I am sure that Simon too had many questions as he came to meet Jesus. We sometimes think that we need to answer all the objections that anyone might have before leading them to the Lord. Andrew did not have all the answers when he first came to Jesus. I am sure that Simon was the same. They found their answers only when they came to the Lord. They came with all their questions and doubts and found their answers in Jesus.

When Jesus met Simon, he changed his name. Jesus told him he would no longer be known as "Simon." He would be called "Cephas," in the Aramaic language, or "Peter," in the Greek language. Both names mean "rock." In Biblical times a name represented the character of the individual. We are not told what Peter was like before he met the Lord Jesus. After his encounter with the Lord Jesus, however, he would become Peter the rock.

What was the significance of this name? Did Jesus name him "the rock" because of what he would endure for the cause of Christ? Later, Peter would speak a lot about suffering in his letters. It may also be possible that Jesus changed Simon's name to represent something that he would become for the church. Peter would become one of the founders of the early church. He would be used of God in a missionary capacity to establish believers. He would become a very in uential figure in the church of the New Testament period.

The Lord Jesus had a purpose for Peter. It was only in coming to Jesus that this purpose could be fulfilled. Andrew played a vital role in that overall plan of God. He introduced Peter to the Lord. You never know what will become of the individuals you introduce to the Lord Jesus. Each of us has a particular role to play in the expansion of the kingdom of God.

The next day Jesus left for Galilee. There he found a man by the name of Philip. Jesus invited Philip to follow him. We are not told how long Philip followed the Lord. Like John and Andrew, however, Philip could not keep what he saw in Jesus to himself. He spoke to a friend named Nathanael and told him that they had found the one of whom Moses spoke—Jesus of Nazareth. There was a natural compulsion on the part of these individuals to share the good news of Jesus with others. Like John the Baptist, they understood that their experience with the Lord was not meant to be kept for themselves. They seemed unable to keep it to themselves. They had to share it with others.

When Nathanael heard that Jesus was from Nazareth, he refused to believe what Philip had told him. He had certain prejudices against this town. "Can anything good come from there?" Nathanael asked Philip (verse 46). Have you ever met people like this? You try to share the Lord with them, but they are so filled with their own preconceived notions that they cannot hear what you are saying. Maybe they have met some hypocritical Christians over the years. Maybe they feel that this "Jesus stuff" is for weaklings. Maybe they have been turned off by an unloving Christian who preached at them about their evil ways without living the life of Christ before them.

Philip was not distracted in his witness because of Nathanael's prejudices. "Come and see," he told Nathanael. That was all he said. He did not try to deal with all Nathanael's objections. He did not try to solve all his problems before bringing him to the Lord. All Philip said was: "Come and see." For some strange reason Nathanael took Philip up on his offer and went with him to meet Jesus. Sometimes that is all that is required. You don't have to answer all objections. You simply have to point people to Jesus. He will do the rest.

What Jesus had to say to Nathanael shattered all his prejudices. Jesus said to Nathanael: "Here is a true Israelite, in whom there is nothing false" (verse 47). What Jesus was saying was something like this: "Nathanael, there is nothing hypocritical about you. You say what you think. You do not believe in me. You are coming to me with all your doubts and prejudices. I know all about them." Nathanael asked Jesus: "How do you know me?" Nathanael was surprised by the direct approach of Jesus. Jesus responded: "I saw you while you were still under the fig tree before Philip called you."

Nathanael was in shock. We do not know what he was doing under that fig tree. Had he been praying? Had he been doing something wrong? We are not told. What is important to note here is that Jesus knew everything about Nathanael. Jesus knew the thoughts of his mind. He knew his every movement. Nathanael's prejudices were shattered. This man Jesus must be the Messiah. "Then Nathanael declared, 'Rabbi, you are the Son of God; you are the King of Israel.'" Jesus told Nathanael, "You shall see greater things than that." Nathanael saw Jesus for himself. When he saw Jesus, he was absolutely convinced Jesus was the Messiah.

Jesus told Nathanael in verse 51 that he would see the angels of God ascending and descending on the Son of Man. The meaning of this verse is debated among commentators. We may interpret it literally. There may have been an occasion, not recorded for us in the gospels, when Nathanael actually saw the angels ministering to the Lord in such a way. It is also possible to understand this verse in a figurative sense. The opening up of the heavens and the angels as messengers of God ascending and descending could clearly be Christ's way of saying to Nathanael that he would reveal many more such matters to him. Christ would open his understanding to the things of God in a way he had never understood before. What is clear in this passage is that the Lord promised Nathanael that he had not finished with him. Nathanael had many unanswered questions. In time the Lord would give him answers.

What does this passage have to say to us today? It reminds us of our responsibility to share the good news of the Lord Jesus Christ with others. Each of these men received an invitation to follow the Lord Jesus Christ. Nathanael came with many doubts. Simon and Andrew came with many unanswered questions. Those who led them to the Lord were not able to answer all their questions. We may not have the answers to the objections thrown at us. We do, however, know someone who can answer these objections.

Many put off coming to the Lord because of unanswered questions. The very fact that they do not come to the only one who can give them an answer means that they never will find the answers they need. Only in him will they, like the disciples, find the answers to these questions.

For Consideration:

• Do we need to have all the answers before pointing someone to the Lord Jesus? What does this passage teach us?

• Do you have the same need to share Christ with those around you? If not, what do you suppose is stopping you from sharing him with your friends and acquaintances?

For Prayer:

• Ask God to show you what hinders you from sharing Christ with others.

• Take a moment to pray for friends or loved ones who are presently in need of the Lord. Ask God to reveal himself to them.

• Ask God to open up an opportunity for you today to share with someone the hope you have in Christ.

4

The Marriage of Cana

Read John 2:1–11

The setting was a wedding in Cana of Galilee. The time was three days after the calling of Nathanael. Jesus, his disciples, and his mother had been invited to the wedding. It was here that Jesus performed his first public miracle.

A problem arose during the wedding. The master of the feast ran out of wine. Have you ever invited someone to your home for a meal and run out of food? You can imagine the embarrassment of this situation. To invite quests to a banquet and not serve them would have been a tremendous insult. The honor of the family was at stake. This would not be very easily forgotten. The master of the banquet was in a difficult situation indeed. Mary, the mother of Jesus, felt a particular need to do something. She came to Jesus with the problem.

Why did Mary come to Jesus? I believe she came to him because she believed he could do something about this embarrassing dilemma. It may have been that this situation came about because of poor planning. Someone had not correctly estimated the amount of wine needed. Have you ever found yourself in difficulty because of a bad decision? You hesitated to go to the Lord because you made such a mess of things. Mary came to Jesus because she had confidence that she could take this problem to the Lord.

Mary has much to teach us here. Do you have the boldness of Mary today? Will you come humbly to the Lord with your failures and pain and ask him to heal you and those you have hurt? Mary had the boldness to come to Jesus.

Jesus' initial response to Mary is puzzling. The King James Version tells us that Jesus responded by saying: "Woman, what have I to do with you? Mine hour is not yet come" (2:4). How are we to understand such a seemingly harsh response by our Lord toward his mother? We need to understand that the term "woman" here is a term of endearment. The New International Version of the Bible translates this by the words "dear woman." What Jesus is saying is something like this: "Dear woman, why are you asking me about it? It is not yet time for me to reveal my power to the world."

Have you ever prayed to the Lord for something and received the answer: "It is not yet time?" What do you do when the Lord gives you this answer? Mary turns to the servants and tells them to do whatever the Lord asks them to do. There is a note of expectation on Mary's part. Though the Lord had not yet answered her prayer, she did not lose heart. She knew he had heard her request. Her faith was not shattered. She left her request with the Lord expecting that in his time, he would answer.

Was it because of Mary's faith that the Lord chose to answer? We do not know. What we do know, however, is that when Mary left, Jesus called on the servants to fill six water pots with water. He did not explain to them why they were to do this. Each of these pots could hold twenty to thirty gallons of water (seventy-five to one hundred fifteen liters). It would have taken some time to fill them.

When the pots were filled, Jesus told the servants to draw water from the pots and give it to the master of the banquet. Have you ever wondered what must have been going through the minds of these servants as they brought this water to the master? They had just filled the pots with water. Jesus was asking them to take water to the master. Would he have appreciated the servants bringing him water as a solution to his problem? What would be his response towards the servants for this cruel joke at his expense?

Mary had told them to do whatever the Lord had commanded, so the servants obeyed. They took the water to the master. It had changed into wine. When the master of the banquet tasted the wine, he discovered that it was a much better wine than the wine his guests had been drinking. Mary was not discouraged when the Lord told her that it was not the right time. She waited on him. Her waiting proved worthwhile. Don't be discouraged if God does not answer your prayer right away. Keep on praying, asking and waiting. In his time, the Lord will answer.

The Bible tells us that the master of the banquet did not know where the wine came from. He assumed that the bridegroom had gotten some from a secret stock he had hidden away somewhere. "You have saved the best till now," he told the bridegroom (verse 10). It seems that only Mary, the servants, and the disciples were fully aware of what had taken place that day.

Not only did Jesus answer Mary's prayer, he exceeded her expectations. They now had all the wine they needed, and the quality of the wine was superior to the wine that they had at first.

What a wonderful God we serve. While man had failed, Jesus came into their failure and worked it all out for good. Not only did he work everything out, the results went far beyond their wildest dreams. This story teaches us something about the grace and compassion of our Lord. He is willing to do far more than you can ask or think. He shows us here that he delights in picking up the broken pieces and making them right again.

Verse 11 tells us that his disciples believed in him that day because of this miracle. While the disciples already believed in the Lord, this miracle confirmed to them that he really was the Son of God. Their faith was strengthened because of what they had seen that day. Not only was the hurt healed, but Jesus received the glory and praise.

Have you failed in your life? Has that failure been an embarrassment to you? This story ought to encourage you to run to the Lord. Don't hesitate to come to him today and tell him your failure. Don't hesitate to ask him to fix it for you. He delights in making things right. He is willing to do more than you could ever imagine.

For Consideration:

• Have you ever failed in your walk with the Lord? What was that failure?

• Were people hurt by your failure? Who?

• Have you ever taken this matter to the Lord for healing?

For Prayer:

• Ask the Lord to forgive you for your failure.

• Ask him to heal both you and those you hurt from the pain caused by this failure.

• Thank him that he is a God of tremendous grace and compassion.

5

The Cleansing of
the Temple

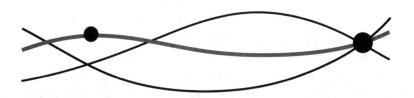

Read John 2:12–25

From Cana of Galilee, Jesus went on to Capernaum and eventually to Jerusalem for the Passover. The Passover was a celebration of the deliverance of the Jews from the bondage of Egypt. The Passover was a yearly celebration. It brought Jews from the surrounding areas to Jerusalem. They came to offer sacrifices to the Lord and to thank him for the deliverance of their people.

Because of the distance traveled, some people chose to purchase the animals required for sacrifice upon arrival in Jerusalem rather than taking the animals with them on the long journey. To buy their sacrificial animals, the people needed to have their money exchanged into the local currency. For this reason the temple was filled with money changers and merchants of cattle, sheep, and doves. These money changers and merchants were an important part of the celebration of the Passover.

You can imagine the scene before the Lord Jesus when he

arrived at the temple in Jerusalem. As he entered the temple, he saw the courtyard filled with cattle, sheep and doves. Maybe he watched the merchants trying to drum up business as they cried out to the passers-by. The money changers had set up their tables and they too were doing business. The scene before him struck a raw nerve with Jesus. He was not pleased with what he saw. The Bible tells us that he made a whip from cords he found in the courtyard and began to drive out the cattle, sheep, and doves. He overturned the tables of the money changers, sending their money ying all over the oor. All around was mass confusion, as the cattle, sheep, and doves ran to and fro, seeking to find a means of escape. The merchants likely chased after their animals. The money changers probably scrambled to gather up the money that had been on the tables the Lord had overturned. As they gathered up the money, they perhaps had to avoid being trampled by the cattle and the merchants running after them to bring them back to their pens. Above all this was the angry voice of the Lord yelling at the merchants and money changers saying: "Get these out of here! How dare you turn my Father's house into a market!" (verse 16).

How do we account for Jesus' attitude here in this passage? Matthew 21:13 may help us understand why Jesus was so angry that day. In this verse Jesus quotes from the Old Testament saying, "My house will be called a house of prayer, but you are making it a 'den of robbers.'"

What did Jesus see when he arrived at the temple that day? He saw the commercialization of a religious holiday. The merchants had come to the celebration of the Passover to make money. The Passover had lost its meaning. It was no longer a time for the celebration of deliverance from Egypt. It was a time to make money at the expense of their brothers and sisters. The fact that Jesus accused them of theft in Matthew 21:13 seems to suggest that they were making an unreasonable profit from their fellow Jews.

How easy it is to look with an accusing eye at these businessmen in the temple. The reality of the matter, however, is that as believers we can be guilty of the same sin. Jesus' concern here was not just money. As he looked over the crowd gathered there that day, he saw people who had come with a variety of motives and intentions. Their focus was not on God. They were there for what they could get themselves. Sometimes we go to church simply because of tradition. Sometimes we go to meet friends. Sometimes we go out of guilt. It grieved the Lord Jesus that the hearts of those present were not stirred at the thought of how much they owed God. Despite his wonderful provision for them, they could not find it in their hearts to worship and praise him. They were not driven by a passion for God.

As the disciples watched the Lord, they remembered what the Psalmist said: "Zeal for your house consumes me." In cleansing the temple, the Lord Jesus fulfilled this prophecy of Psalm 69:9. The Lord Jesus is concerned about what goes on behind the walls of our churches. He is concerned about hypocrisy. Nowhere else in the gospels do we see the Lord react with such anger. A quick look at the gospels reveals to us that while Jesus showed great patience with the sinner, he spoke harshly to the religious hypocrite. Hypocrisy was something that angered the Lord.

The Jewish leaders present that day came to Jesus to ask him by what authority he was doing these things. They asked for a sign to prove his authority. They were looking for his credentials. If he was from God, he would be able to prove this by demonstrating the power of God in some clear way. Jesus told them that he would destroy the temple and raise it up again in three days.

The Jews thought that Jesus was referring to the actual temple building. This indeed would be an impressive feat. They reminded him that it took forty-six years to build the temple. Jesus, however, was not referring to the physical temple. He was speaking about his own body. His body would be laid down in death. Evil people would destroy it, but he would rise from the dead in three days. His crucifixion and resurrection would be the miracle that would prove his authority. Only the promised Messiah could accomplish this.

By the many miracles he performed while in Jerusalem, Jesus also proved to these leaders that he had been given authority by the Father. Many men and women believed in him because of the miracles they saw him do. Verse 24 tells us that though these individuals believed in him because of the miracles, Jesus did not entrust himself to them. To entrust yourself to someone is to place that person in your confidence. Why would Jesus not reveal himself fully to those who believed in him? These people were prepared to follow him as long as Jesus healed the sick and fed the hungry. They believed in him as a miracle worker but not as their Savior. Jesus knew their hearts. He knew that, like the money changers and the merchants in the temple, the people too were only concerned about themselves and getting all they could out of Jesus.

This attitude hindered the Lord from revealing himself to the people of that day. Maybe it's time to examine our lives and motives. Maybe it's time for us to search our hearts to see if there is anything that blocks him from entrusting himself more fully to us.

For Consideration:

• Are there motives or attitudes that the Lord has been revealing to you in this meditation that do not bring glory to his name? What are they?

• Has Jesus entrusted himself to you? What does it mean to have Jesus entrust himself to us?

- What were the attitudes of those who served in the temple that day? What was the attitude of the people? Have you ever wrestled with these same attitudes?

For Prayer:

- Ask the Lord to show you if there are any obstacles blocking intimacy with him today.

- Ask God to reveal your true motives and intentions in service for him.

- Thank him that he is faithful to us even when we have been found guilty.

6

Born Again

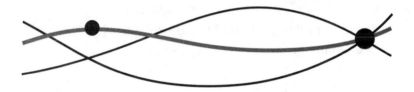

Read John 3:1–10

The term "born again" has come to mean something other than what it was intended to mean. Secular society has picked up on the term and used it to their advantage. The term originates from a discussion between a Pharisee named Nicodemus and the Lord Jesus. It is one of the most important of all Bible doctrines. We will examine what it means to be born again in this meditation.

After the cleansing of the temple, Jesus remained in the city of Jerusalem. John 2:23 tells us that he performed many miracles in Jerusalem during those days. Many people believed in him because of these miracles. One of these people was a man by the name of Nicodemus. We learn some important things about Nicodemus in John 3:1–2.

First, we learn that Nicodemus was a Pharisee. The Pharisees were the foremost religious leaders of the day. They had a powerful in uence on the people. They were characterized by their rigorous practice of the Law of Moses.

To keep from breaking the precious laws of Moses, they added some of their own lesser laws. Nicodemus, as a man of the Pharisees, was a very careful observer of the Law of Moses. He was a "religious" man.

Second, we notice that Nicodemus came to Jesus (verse 2). He obviously had questions that needed to be answered. He came to Jesus to find those answers. He had seen Jesus perform his wonderful miracles. He had no doubt that these miracles proved that Jesus was from God. He wanted to know more.

Third, we notice that Nicodemus came to Jesus at night. We know that the attitude of the Pharisees towards Jesus was not good. The Pharisees wanted to get rid of Jesus. In John 9 they put a blind man out of the synagogue because he believed that Jesus was from God. Nicodemus risked much by his association with the Lord Jesus. If it was discovered that he came to Jesus, he risked his position as a respected man among the Pharisees. Should he go to Jesus with his questions and risk being caught? His need for answers was so strong that he took this risk. He went at night, however, when there was less chance of being discovered.

Fourth, we learn that Nicodemus told Jesus that he knew he was from God. The miracles he had seen Jesus do had convinced him of this.

Nicodemus was a man who lived an exemplary life. He loved and very carefully observed the Law of Moses. He was also a man who had a burning desire to learn more about the Lord Jesus. He risked his position as a respected man of the community to come to sit at Jesus' feet. Nicodemus also believed that Jesus was from God. He could not close his mind to the facts he saw. He allowed the miracles of Jesus to speak to his heart. What more could you ask for in believers but that they be people who love and obey the Word of God, desire deeply to be in the presence of the

Lord, and hold tightly to the conviction that Jesus is truly a "teacher come from God" ? (verse 2 NKJV).

Notice what Jesus said to Nicodemus when he saw him come: "No one can see the kingdom of God unless he is born again" (verse 3). How would you have felt if you were Nicodemus? Nicodemus had felt all along that he would enter the kingdom of heaven because of his good life and beliefs. He felt that his future was assured. Jesus was telling him something else. Jesus was telling him that unless he was "born again," he would never see that kingdom of God.

Nicodemus could not understand what Jesus was telling him. He felt that Jesus was referring to a physical birth. He asked Jesus how he could be born again now that he was old. In answer to this, Jesus told Nicodemus that unless a man was born of water and the Spirit, he could not enter the kingdom of heaven.

An unborn child lives in the uid of the mother's womb. When the time is right, that uid is expelled and the child is born. A sure sign that the child is ready to be born is the "breaking of the water." Being "born of water" refers to physical birth. Jesus did not stop here, however. He told Nicodemus that this physical birth was not enough. "Unless a man is born of water *and* the Spirit," said Jesus, he will not enter the kingdom of God (verse 5, emphasis added). Jesus was telling Nicodemus that there is more than one birth. There is a physical birth that places us in this world (born of water) and there is also a spiritual birth that places us into the kingdom of God (born of the Spirit).

Let us continue to use the illustration of birth to understand what Jesus was saying here. Before the moment of conception, the womb of the mother is unproductive. Life begins in that unproductive womb when the sperm fertilizes the egg. The woman is not capable of producing life by herself. Her egg must be fertilized by the man's sperm.

When the egg is fertilized, new life begins and the mother, over a period of nine months, experiences physical and emotional changes as that new life grows in her.

Spiritual birth is, in many ways, like this physical birth. The soul of an individual, like the womb of the woman, is barren and unfruitful. The soul of the person is dead. For this new spiritual life to begin, it must be planted in the soul by God. This is what takes place at the time of our spiritual birth. The Spirit of God places his own life into our souls. Once implanted in us by our willing acceptance of it, this new life begins to grow within us. We quickly see the results in our lives. The new nature needs to be fed. It produces in us a desire for the things of God. Our lives change. We are aware of a new life and a new appetite within us. The things we used to enjoy, we no longer desire. We have a deep craving now for the things of God.

"Flesh gives birth to esh," said Jesus, "but the Spirit gives birth to spirit" (verse 6). Your physical birth will not get you into the kingdom of God. By your physical birth, you become a child of this earth. By your spiritual birth, you become a child of God. If you want to see the kingdom of heaven, you must be born again.

How can a person be born again? This is the work of the Spirit of God. Like the wind, the Spirit blows where he pleases. Like the wind, the Spirit's movements are unpredictable. When he blows on your soul, however, though you do not see him, you know his presence.

My wife and I lived for a number of years on the islands of Mauritius and Reunion in the Indian Ocean. When we heard that a cyclone was coming, we brought everything inside. We closed all the shutters and locked ourselves in the house until the cyclone had passed. We did not dare open the shutters until we were assured that the storm was over. We often treat the Spirit of God like this. When the Spirit of God speaks to your heart, don't close the shutters of your heart. Open your heart and let him blow into your life. Let him sweep away what does not honor the Lord. Let him change those things that need to be changed. Sometimes opening our lives to the Lord Jesus is a scary thing. We are afraid of what will happen. Unless the Spirit of God blows on our hearts and plants his life in our souls, however, we will never see the kingdom of God. If the life of the Spirit of God is not living in us, we do not belong to God. Paul tells us in Romans 8:9 that if we do not have the Spirit of God living in us, we do not belong to the Lord Jesus.

How can you tell if you have experienced this new birth? Once you were dead to spiritual matters, but now you are aware of the life of Christ pounding through your spiritual veins. Once there was no appetite for Christ, but now you cannot get enough of him. The changes will become evident not only to yourself but also to all those around you.

Nicodemus, as a leader of the people of God, had never been born again. He was trying to point others to heaven when he was not going there himself. Only those who have been born into the family of God by this spiritual birth are the children of God. As religious as Nicodemus was, without a spiritual birth, he would not see the kingdom of God.

For Consideration:

- What things do people depend on to try to get to heaven?

- What is the new birth? Why is the new birth necessary?

- What evidence is there of this new birth in your life?

For Prayer:

- If you know the reality of this new birth, take a moment to thank the Lord for what he has been doing in your life.

- Take a moment to pray for people you know who, like Nicodemus, have been trying to get to heaven in their own strength. Ask God to reveal to them the clear teaching of Christ on the new birth. Ask God to give you an opportunity to point them to this new birth.

7

The Lifting up of the Son of Man

Read John 3:11–21

The conversation with Nicodemus continues here in this next section. Jesus had explained to Nicodemus the importance of being born again. Nicodemus, as a spiritual leader, did not understand what Jesus was telling him. He had never experienced this new birth.

This next section begins with Jesus' statement to Nicodemus: "I tell you the truth, we speak of what we know, and we testify to what we have seen, but still you people do not accept our testimony" (verse 11). What was Jesus saying here in this verse?

Who was Jesus referring to when he used the word "we" in this passage? Some propose that the "we" is Jesus and his disciples. The problem, however, is that at this time the disciples themselves did not have a clear knowledge of what Jesus taught. This has led others to propose that the "we" of this passage is Jesus and the prophets who had prophesied about him. In the context of this passage, however, we discover that the Lord Jesus has just been speaking of the Holy Spirit, who, like the wind, blows where he desires. (See verse 8.) It may be more likely that Jesus is saying to Nicodemus that both he and the Holy Spirit had come to bear witness to the heavenly things they had seen. Who else but the Lord Jesus and the Holy Spirit of God could testify to the "things they had seen and heard"?

Jesus told Nicodemus that though he and the Holy Spirit had testified to the spiritual leaders of Israel of what they had seen and heard, they refused to listen. God himself had spoken, but they did not recognize his voice. Nicodemus and his co-workers were the leaders of Israel. They represented the elite of God's people, yet they could not hear.

Nicodemus was blinded to the spiritual things of God. Jesus had spoken to him in simple earthly language. He had used the illustration of birth and the wind to explain to Nicodemus what it meant to be born again and enter the kingdom of heaven. Nicodemus, despite these illustrations, could not understand what Jesus was saying. Jesus was saying something like this: If you cannot understand these things when I illustrate them in earthly terms, how could you possibly understand if I spoke to you on a deeper spiritual level? "No one has ever gone into heaven except the one who came from heaven—the Son of Man" (verse 13). He alone can explain these matters to you. He alone has full understanding of the things of God. You cannot understand these matters because you are of this world.

In order to explain more fully to Nicodemus what it meant to enter the kingdom of heaven, Jesus used another illustration. He had already used the illustration of physical birth and the wind, but Nicodemus had not understood. He then used a spiritual illustration. He gave him an illustration from the Old Testament Scriptures: "Just as Moses lifted up the snake in the desert, so the Son of Man must be lifted up, that everyone who believes in him may have eternal life" (verses 14–15).

This illustration came from Numbers 21:4–9. The people of God were in the wilderness. They were growing weary of the manna they had been eating every day. They were running short of water. They spoke out against Moses and God. In his anger, the Lord sent poison snakes into their camp. These snakes bit the people and many of them died. The people who remained cried out to Moses to help them. They confessed their sin and pleaded: "Pray that the Lord will take the snakes away from us" (Numbers 21:7). Moses prayed to the Lord. The Lord told him to make a snake out of brass and put it on a pole. Anyone who looked to that snake would be healed. Jesus reminded Nicodemus of this story. Like that snake of Moses' day, Jesus would be lifted up for all to see. Only those who looked to him and believed would be healed of their sin.

There are many people who believe that the Lord Jesus died on the cross. Satan himself does not doubt this historical fact. It was not enough for the people in the days of Moses to recognize that there was a brass snake hanging on a pole. They had to believe that their only hope of healing was to be found in looking to that brass snake. They had to come to that snake with a repentant heart, recognizing that they had blasphemed the name of the Lord. They needed to realize that, without this provision of God, they would die of the poison in their veins.

This is how we need to come to the cross. It is not enough to recognize that the cross was a historical fact that took place many years ago. We need to come to the cross like the people of Moses' day came to the pole. Just as those who looked at the snake on a pole were healed physically, those who look to the Lord Jesus lifted up on a cross for their sins will be healed spiritually. Without the cross, we too will die in our sin. There is no other way to be saved from the poison of sin that circulates in our veins. Jesus alone, by his death and shed blood, can save us from the wrath of God. We need to look to the cross as though our very lives depended on it.

John 3:16 is the best known verse of the entire Bible. God proves both his love and his justice in this verse. He proves that he is just in punishing evil. He proves that he is love by taking that punishment himself. He sent his Son to die in our places. The death of the Lord Jesus satisfied the justice of God. All that remains for us is to place our confidence in the death he died. We must recognize that the Lord Jesus died for each one of us personally. The death of the Lord Jesus does not save the whole world. It saves only those who believe. We must claim his death as our own. When we stand before the judgment seat of Christ on the last day, our entrance into the kingdom of heaven will be based on the fact that the Lord Jesus personally paid for our sin. He put it on his own account. We cling to the cross of the Lord Jesus as our only hope of eternal life. We recognize that Jesus needed to die for us.

Notice here in verses 15 and16 that Jesus clearly tells us that those who believe on him and his work have everlasting life. It is not something they will have someday. They already have it. Jesus did not come to condemn the world. He came to offer forgiveness and life. To refuse to believe in him, however, is to perish. If we have not placed our absolute confidence and trust in him, we are already condemned. The poison of sin ows even now through our veins. There is only one cure for this sin. The Lord Jesus alone, by his work on the cross, has provided a means of escape. Only by looking to him can we be cured.

Verse 19 reminds us that though God sent his Son into the world to save the world, the world rejected him. He came to offer his light to them, but people chose the darkness. Like a bug under an overturned stone running for the cover of darkness, we ran from him and his offer of salvation. What an insult to the Son of God. He came to set us free from the condemnation of sin. He came to take on himself the penalty for our sin, but we turned our backs on him and his offer.

Jesus concluded his conversation with Nicodemus by stating that those who do evil hate the light and will not come to it lest their deeds be exposed. These who live in sin are slaves to sin. They do not want to give up their sin. They do not want to come to the Lord Jesus because they love their evil. These people will perish because they refuse to come to the light and discover who they really are. Their pride will destroy them. They would rather live in the dark than to come to the light and face the truth of their sin.

Those who live in the truth, however, are very different. (See verse 21.) Not only do they come to the light but the light of God dwells in them. This light produces fruit in their lives. They know the power of the light of God working in them. They know his presence in their daily walk. Has this been your experience?

The cross of the Lord Jesus is our only hope of eternal life. It is never easy to have the light expose our sin. Many people have chosen to run from this light. These people still live in the dark. If you want to know the truth, you must first allow the light to expose you for who you really are. Let his light shine on you. Let his Word reveal the hidden motives of your heart. The Son of Man lifted up on that awful cross is our only hope of eternal salvation. Look to him and live.

For Consideration:

• Why is it so hard for many people to recognize their need of a Savior?

• Can people believe that Jesus died on the cross without ever trusting in Jesus' work on that cross for their eternal life?

For Prayer:

- Take a moment to thank the Lord for his provision for your salvation.

- Do you have friends or loved ones who have never accepted the Lord's provision for their salvation? Take a moment right now to pray for them.

8

Jesus versus John

Read John 3:22–36

Have you ever experienced a tinge of jealousy when you saw how the Lord was blessing someone else? If we are honest with ourselves, we have to admit that jealousy is something we all have to deal with. John 3:22–36 gives us much to consider when it comes to the question of jealousy.

After his conversation with Nicodemus, Jesus left Jerusalem for the Judean countryside. Verse 22 tells us that Jesus spent time here with his disciples. People came to him to be baptized. (John 4:2 states that Jesus himself did not baptize anyone, but his disciples did the work.) John the Baptist was also baptizing people in that same general area (verse 23). It should be understood here that the baptism of John was a means of pointing men and women to the Lord Jesus. John's baptism, like the baptism of Christ, called people to repentance and faith in the Messiah.

It is important to note that John had a very successful

ministry. Scripture tells us that people were "constantly coming" to be baptized by John (verse 23). John was seeing great things happening in his ministry. His ministry was blessed of God. These were exciting times for John and his disciples.

John's ministry was not without its difficulties, however. On one occasion an argument developed between John's disciples and the Jews (verse 25). The argument revolved around the issue of purification or ceremonial washing. We are not told what caused this argument. It seems, however, from the context that the issue that started this debate was the baptism of John. According to the Old Testament laws, if Jews defiled themselves in some way, they would offer a sacrifice for forgiveness and then either bathe in water or be ceremonially sprinkled to cleanse themselves from their impurities (Numbers 19). It may be that the Jews were confusing John's baptism with the Jewish ceremony of purification. While we do not know the details of this debate, we do understand that John's ministry was being opposed. We can be sure that if God is blessing our ministry, there will be opposition. In this case the opposition came from the religious people of the land. It could be that these Jewish leaders were jealous of the number of people coming to be baptized by John.

As John and the Jewish leaders were debating the question of purification, some of John's disciples came to him with yet another problem. It had come to their attention that the Lord Jesus was in the area and people were going to him to be baptized. This greatly concerned the disciples of John. They saw this as a threat.

Have you ever had someone leave your church to go to another? How do you feel when someone else is able to minister where you failed? John's disciples were jealous. They resented anything that would break up their following and keep it from growing. People were leaving them to follow Jesus. Maybe they wondered how they could get these people back.

While the reaction of the disciples of John was one of jealousy and competition, it is important to see the response of John himself. Scripture tells us four things in verses 27–30 that will help us as we deal with the feeling of jealousy in our lives.

John first told his disciples that "a man can only receive what is given to him from heaven" (verse 27). John recognized here that all things come from God. Even this perceived problem they were dealing with now came from heaven. John was content to accept whatever the Lord God was doing in his life.

When you are tempted to jealousy as you look at what God is doing for someone else, consider that it is God who has blessed these individuals. When you feel that you should be seeing greater fruit in your life and ministry, remember that you can only be as fruitful as God himself allows you to be. John had learned to accept God's purposes for his life. How often have we set our own goals and agendas? We become frustrated when we do not see things happening the way we want. How much blessing and fruitfulness have we missed because we have never learned to be content with what we have received from God? Can you be content only to be what God has intended for you to be? Jealousy is often the result of trying to be something other than what God has intended us to be.

Second, notice in verse 28 that John reminded his disciples that he was not the Christ but was sent ahead of him to announce his coming. He was called to be a servant of Christ. He understood his role. Each of us has a role to play. Each of us has a ministry. John knew his place and was happy to do what the Lord had called him to do. He was not the Christ. He was his messenger. John wanted to be the best messenger he could be for him. He was happy in this role.

How easy it is to look at the ministries and gifts of others and want what they have. God calls us to be content with our own particular calling in life. Whether our calling is humble or great, we need to learn to be content with what God has chosen for us.

Third, John shared with his disciples an example from everyday life to explain to them how he felt about the Lord Jesus receiving the glory. He used an example of a groom and his best man. Have you ever been the best man at a friend's wedding? What are your thoughts at that moment? Doesn't your heart explode with joy and happiness? This is his day. All eyes are focused on the groom and the bride. No one seems to notice the best man. No one comes to congratulate the best man for having been chosen to stand beside the groom. All attention is on the groom. As the best man, you would not have it any other way. The best man feels no jealousy for the happiness of the groom. He feels only joy in his heart for his friend on the day of his wedding.

This was John's experience. He had been sent ahead of the Lord to prepare the way. Like the best man, he waited for the coming of the groom. When the Lord Jesus appeared, John experienced only joy and contentment. Yes, all eyes were taken away from John and focused on the Lord, but that was how it should be. John would not have had it any other way. His heart over owed with joy, for this was the day of the Lord.

Fourth, John reminded his disciples that he needed to "become less" so that the Lord Jesus could "become greater" (verse 30). John understood that his ministry was to point people to the Lord Jesus. John wanted people to see the Lord. What an insult it is to the Lord Jesus when we take for ourselves the glory he rightly deserves. Like John, we are to be servants who de ect all glory to the Lord Jesus. When John accepted his calling from God, he committed himself to lifting up the name of the Lord Jesus. He willingly died to himself and his own glory. As servants of Christ, our role is to point people to him. This is our purpose. It also ought to be our delight.

John concluded his discussion with his disciples in verses 31–36 by telling them who Jesus really was. "He who comes from above is above all," said John (verse 31 NKJV). Jesus was from heaven itself. He has the authority over all things. He is the King of Kings. He controls all things. "He testifies to what he has seen and heard" (verse 32). What Jesus spoke he did not receive from someone else. He spoke from personal experience. No one else could speak as he spoke. No one else had experienced heaven and knew the purpose and plan of the Father as he did. Jesus spoke the very words of God. He gave the Holy Spirit without measure (verse 34). The Father loves Jesus and has committed all things into his hands (verse 35). Jesus acts in all things on the Father's behalf. The care and control of the universe is in his hands. To believe in him is to have eternal life. To reject him is to fall under the judgment and wrath of the Father (verse 36).

Is there any wonder why John the Baptist experienced no jealousy at the thought that the Lord Jesus' disciples were baptizing more people than he? The problem with the disciples of John was that they did not really understand who Jesus was. To understand who Jesus is, is to bow willingly in submission to him. To understand who he is, is to say with your whole heart: "He must become greater; I must become less." May God give us the attitude of John.

For Consideration:

- Take a moment to consider the last time you experienced jealousy. What does the example of John teach you about the real cause of this jealousy?

- Consider the principles learned here in this meditation. What particular principle learned here in this meditation do you find particularly helpful in your struggle with jealousy?

- What does this passage have to say to you about the attitude you ought to have when things don't seem to be going the way you would like?

For Prayer:

- Ask the Lord to forgive you for jealousy experienced in your life.

- Ask him to help you to be content with his role for you.

- Take a moment to thank the Lord for someone else's ministry and gifts (particularly someone whose ministry and gifts you tend to envy).

9

The Samaritan Woman

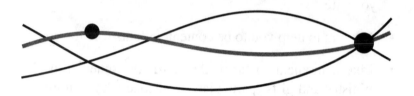

Read John 4:1–42

Whaat kind of person can the Lord use? You do not have to have a theological education to be used of God. You do not have to have many years of experience. The Lord can use you just as you are. This story of the Samaritan woman is a very beautiful example of this.

Jesus' disciples were baptizing those who came to them in the Judean countryside. The Pharisees heard what Jesus was doing. In chapter 3 we saw that the Pharisees had attacked the ministry of John the Baptist. This sort of encounter was neither helpful nor desirable. Jesus decided to avoid contact with the Pharisees, and so he left the region.

The Lord decided to go to Galilee. The most direct route to Galilee was through Samaria. The Jews would not travel through the region of Samaria because of their hatred for the Samaritans. The Jews of Jesus' day would choose instead to take a longer route which bypassed this region. In verse 4 we read that Jesus "had to go through Samaria". God obviously had a plan for this region.

Our Lord came to a town in Samaria called Sychar (verse 5). The town of Sychar was near a plot of land that Jacob had given to his son Joseph. Jacob's well was in that region. This well had great historical value.

Jesus sat down by the well to rest while the disciples went into town to buy food. It was about noon when Jesus arrived at the well. A woman came to the well as Jesus was resting. It is important to note several things about this individual. First, she was a woman. According to Jewish etiquette, it was not proper for a man to speak to a woman in public. By speaking to this woman, the Lord was breaking a cultural tradition. When the disciples returned from the town, they were surprised to see their master speaking to a woman. (See verse 27.)

The second thing we should note here is that this woman was a Samaritan. From verse 9 we understand that the Jews had no dealings with the Samaritans. We have already mentioned that the average Jew chose to walk the extra distance around the region of Samaria rather than come into contact with one of these despised people. Jesus did not have this same feeling toward the Samaritans.

Third, this woman had had five husbands and was presently living with a man who was not her husband. (See verses 16–18.) This tells us something about the woman. What had happened to her five husbands? While the Bible does not tell us, it would be too incredible to believe that they had all died. The fact that she was living with a man she was not married to suggests that this woman was not a moral woman. It would be more likely to assume that this woman had been divorced several times. She obviously had trouble keeping a relationship.

Here before Jesus was a troubled woman. She had gone through five husbands. She had not committed herself to marrying the man she was living with. Did she feel lonely? Did she feel rejected? Was she confused? Did she feel insecure? We can only guess.

Jesus began his conversation with the woman by asking her for a drink. The Samaritan woman was surprised to see that Jesus would talk to her. She expressed this to the Lord (verse 9). In so doing, she reminded him of the rift between the Jews and the Samaritans.

The Lord responded by telling her that if she really knew who he was, she would be the one asking him for something to drink. He also had water to give her. His water, however, was living water. The assumption here was that the water he would give her was better than the water she would draw from Jacob's well. (See verse 10.)

The woman seemed offended at this suggestion. Is it possible that she saw here an insult against her race? What is clear is that she took offence at what Jesus was telling her. "Are you greater than our father Jacob, who gave us the well?" she asked (verse 12).

The Lord explained to her the difference between the water that Jacob gave and the water that he would give her. "The water I give . . . will become . . . a spring of water welling up to eternal life," said Jesus (verse 14). He was referring to the salvation that he had to offer. Salvation is like living water. Without water we would surely die. Without water there can only be barrenness and unfruitfulness. The salvation that the Lord offers us, like water, quenches the thirsty soul and brings life and fruitfulness. Whoever drinks of the water of salvation that the Lord offers will never thirst again.

Many around us feel this thirst. They feel unfilfilled and that life has lost its meaning. They are living in a barren desert and need the living water of salvation. The spiritual water that the Lord gives will quench the soul's thirst like nothing else. Only this living water will satisfy us as we drink deeply of it. It is offered to everyone without charge.

The Samaritan woman did not really understand what Jesus was saying. "Give me . . . this water so that I won't . . . have to keep coming here to draw water," she responded (verse 15). She was still thinking about physical water. She had not yet understood the Lord.

To help her understand, Jesus asked her to call her husband. This was where she was hurting. This would have struck a raw nerve with the woman. "I have no husband," she told the Lord (verse 17). "You are right," said Jesus, "you have had five husbands, and the man you now have is not your husband (verses 17–18). She could not hide from the Lord. In bringing this issue up to the woman, Jesus was making her aware of her need for the living water that he had to offer her. This water would heal the hurts in her life. Had she been trying to hide her hurts by having these relationships with the men in her life? The water Jesus offered her would heal the loneliness, emptiness, and insecurity she felt as a woman. Jesus knew her need. He pointed her need out to her to help her understand what he was offering her.

This statement of Jesus shocked the woman. She understood now that he was no mere Jew. Here before her was a prophet. The only way this man could have known these things about her was if God revealed them to him.

Having understood that Jesus was a prophet, the woman tried to divert the attention from herself to the differences between the Jews and the Samaritans. She brought up the age-old debate between the two groups, regarding where God wanted his people to worship him.

Jesus was not distracted by this diversion. Jesus explained that the time was coming when geography would no longer be a concern in worship. God was concerned more about the attitude of the heart than the location of worship. Jesus told her that true worshipers are concerned about worshiping God "in spirit and in truth" (verse 24).

There are many people who give intellectual assent to the truths of the Lord. They enjoy theology, but their spirit is not moved. True worship takes place when our spirits communicate with the Spirit of God. True worship comes from a heart that has been moved by the Spirit of God. True worship is Spirit-led and fueled by the truth of the Word of God. It touches our hearts and souls and draws us into the very presence of God.

The Samaritan woman, though touched by the wisdom of the Lord's response, did not accept what he told her. She stated that when the Messiah came, he would explain these things. "I who speak to you am he," said Jesus (verse 26). This statement must have come as a real shock to the woman. There was something about what Jesus said, however, that broke every ounce of resistance she had. She had been fighting with him all this time, but when she heard what Jesus said, she dropped her water jugs and ran into town. She told her friends to come and see someone who could quite possibly be the Messiah. The people of the town, wanting to see for themselves what the woman was speaking about, made their way to the well where Jesus was resting (verse 30).

In the meantime, the disciples had returned from their shopping trip in town. When they offered the Lord something to eat, he told them that he had food they did not know about (verse 32). This perplexed the disciples. They did not understand what Jesus was talking about. Like the Samaritan woman, they thought he was speaking in the physical sense. Jesus, however, was referring to spiritual food. His food was to do the will of his Father. He had just had an opportunity to witness to the Samaritan woman. This had satisfied his soul.

Have you ever known the satisfaction of serving the

Lord? What a delight it is to be able to serve him. There is nothing more satisfying than to know that you have been used of the Lord in the life of someone else. Serving the Lord brings blessing. There is no Christian so starved as the Christian who does not know the blessing of serving the Lord.

Jesus understood that his encounter with this woman was only the beginning of something great. He told the disciples that there was a great harvest to be brought in. They had not worked for it, but they would reap what other people had sown. In just a short time, they would be rejoicing. (See verses 35–38.) The disciples did not understand what Jesus was saying.

The harvest Jesus spoke about came quickly. Within a few moments of the disciples' return from town, Jacob's well was surrounded by Samaritan seekers. They came with many questions. They came because the Samaritan woman had invited them to come. They listened intently to what Jesus was telling them. The Spirit of God moved among them and they believed in Jesus (verse 39). No longer did they believe because of the Samaritan woman. They believed because of what Jesus had told them. They invited him to stay with them. For two days Jesus and his disciples stayed in Samaria, preaching and teaching the Word of God (verse 40). That day they experienced one of the first New Testament revivals.

How did this revival begin? It began when a Samaritan woman was confronted by the truth about Jesus and her sinful ways. She did not have the time to deal with and confess her sins. She went to her friends, just as she was, and told them what she had heard. God wonderfully touched many lives through this woman.

God can use anyone he chooses. He does not need a man or woman of great ability and skill. God can accomplish as much through someone like the simple Samaritan woman as he can through an educated preacher or teacher of the Word. God can use you just as you are. Won't you surrender yourself to him and let him use you? You will be surprised at what he will do.

For Consideration:

- Are there people in your community like this Samaritan woman (lonely, unloved, and unwanted)? Would you be willing to reach out to them?

- Is there any way in which the church of our day has become like the Jews of Jesus' day (sectarian, proud, etc.)?

- What does this section teach us about placing our confidence in our gifts, education, or experience?

- What kind of person can God use today?

For Prayer:

- Does the Samaritan woman remind you of anyone in your community? Take a moment to pray for a "modern-day Samaritan."

- Ask God to give you the humility of Jesus to reach out to those who are not lovely in the eyes of this world.

- Thank the Lord that he can use you just as you are.

10

The Royal Official's Son

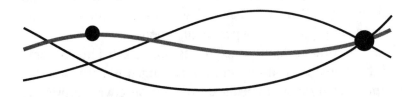

Read John 4:43–54

Jesus had spent two days in the region of Samaria. A great revival had broken out in that land. One can only imagine the excitement that was in the air. The disciples themselves would have been encouraged to see what was taking place. Their faith would have been strengthened as they saw the Samaritans come to personal faith in the Lord. Also, their prejudices would have been confronted by seeing that God actually had a gracious plan for this group of people who were so hated by the Jews.

From Samaria the Lord moved to the region of Galilee. This had been his original destination, according to John 4:3. Matthew 13:54–58 tells us that Jesus had not been accepted in his own country and could not do many great works in that region. Verse 44 indicates that he had originally left Judea because, as a prophet, he had no honor in his own country. What a different response he received from the Samaritans when he stopped there on his way to Galilee. They openly accepted him and many believed in his name.

Verse 45 tells us that the Galileans welcomed Jesus. It appears that they had seen him do many miracles at the Passover Feast in Jerusalem. His fame was spreading. In verse 46 we see that Jesus and his disciples returned to Cana in Galilee where Jesus had turned the water into wine. Some sixteen miles away (twenty-five kilometers) in the town of Capernaum lived a royal official whose son was sick and about to die. This official had heard about Jesus and his miracles. When he heard that Jesus was in the area, he decided to speak to him personally about his son.

The official approached Jesus and asked him to come to his home to heal his son. He explained to Jesus that his son was very close to death. Jesus' response was surprising: "Unless you people see miraculous signs and wonders, . . . you will never believe" (verse 48). Was Jesus addressing the royal official here? This would not seem to be the case. The nobleman came to Jesus with a real burden on his heart. He desperately wanted to see his son healed. Jesus was his last hope. To whom was Jesus speaking when he said: "Unless you people see miraculous signs and wonders, . . . you will never believe"? It may be that Jesus said this because of the Galileans around him who were hoping to be entertained by yet another miracle. You will recall from verse 45 that the reason the Galileans were so quick to accept Jesus was because of the miracles and signs they had seen him do in Jerusalem.

How exciting it would have been for the crowd to hear the nobleman's request. They had heard of Jesus' miracles. Is it possible that many of them had followed him with the hope that they would witness this power at work? Here was the ideal occasion for them to see one of these miracles. Jesus knew the attitude of the people. He was not about to do a miracle simply to entertain the crowd. He rebuked them for their unbelief and the attitude of their hearts. As Jesus was addressing the crowd, the official interrupted him saying: "Sir, come down before my child dies" (verse 49). Jesus was not in a hurry. He had everything under control. He told the official to go home, because his son would live (verse 50).

The Lord does not go to the royal official's home. Had he gone to his home, the crowd would have followed. They would have been there simply to witness his power at work and be entertained by his miracle. Jesus was not interested in making a great show of his power. He healed the boy at a distance. The crowd would not see this miracle. Because of their unbelief, Jesus refused to show them his power. They did not see the power of God at work that day. They were interested in the miracles but not in the person of Christ and the welfare of this young boy who was dying.

As for the royal official, when Jesus told him to return home, he did so, believing that it would be as the Lord said. He went home with the assurance that something good had happened. He returned with the confidence that the Lord had heard his request and would heal his son. There was no ashy show of power. There was no thunderbolt out of heaven. Jesus did not even go to his house. This miracle would take place in a very quiet and private way.

As the royal official returned home, his servant came to meet him with the news that his son was well. When he inquired about the time his son had become well, he discovered that it was at the exact time that Jesus told him to return home.

God's ways are not our ways. We don't know what the nobleman expected when he went to see Jesus. He wanted Jesus to come with him. Jesus did not do this. The crowd was very likely looking forward to seeing a real display of Jesus' power. Again Jesus disappointed them. Jesus was more concerned about people here than he was about demonstrations of power.

There is something else about this story that we need to understand. While Jesus did not do things the way the royal official expected, he did return home in obedience with faith in his heart that he had been heard. Could it be that you too, like this nobleman, already have the answer to your prayer? How foolish it would have been for the official to continue pleading with Jesus to come to his house to heal his son when his prayer had already been answered. Sometimes we look for a sign we already have. The only sign the nobleman needed was the word of Jesus to go home because his son would live. What more did he need? There are people today who are waiting for a thunderbolt from heaven before coming to the Lord or stepping out in obedience to the Lord. Have you heard his gentle voice? That is all you need. Like the royal official, simply step out in obedience and trust the Lord to carry you through.

For Consideration:

- What sort of things do you think hinder the powerful working of the Lord today?

- Why do we become so focused on signs and wonders? Why is it hard to simply take God at his Word?

- Is it possible that you already have the answer to a prayer you have been bringing before the Lord? Could it be that you have been blinded to the answer to this prayer because you have been expecting a different answer?

For Prayer:

- Ask God to forgive you for demanding that he answer your prayers in a certain way.

- Surrender yourself to the will of God. Ask him to help you to accept the plans he has for you, even though they may not be the same as your plans.

- Thank God that he demonstrates to us here that he is concerned about our practical needs.

11

The Healing of the Invalid

Read John 5:1–15

The setting is the city of Jerusalem in Judea. Jesus had come to Jerusalem for a special Jewish feast. The city of Jerusalem harbored his greatest enemies, but Jesus did not allow this to hinder him. On this particular occasion, our Lord went to a pool located by one of the gates to the city of Jerusalem. The sick and disabled gathered around this pool. They believed that its waters had healing power. It was believed that the angel of the Lord would come down from heaven and stir up the waters, and the first person into the pool after the waters were stirred would be healed (verse 4 KJV).

Among those gathered at the pool was a man who had been sick for thirty-eight years. Verse 14 may indicate that this infirmity was the result of sin this man had committed. We should not assume from this that all sickness is the result of some sin that we have committed. There are many other passages of Scripture that would indicate that this is not the case (John 9:3; Job 1:8; Luke 13:2–3). In this particular case, however, there seems to be a connection between the sin of this man and the sickness he was experiencing.

When Jesus saw the man lying there he approached him and asked him if he wanted to get well (verse 6). The man told Jesus that there was no one to help him into the pool when the water was stirred. He was alone in life. Where were his friends and family? They were not there for him in his time of need. He had been left to fend for himself. The Lord Jesus was moved with compassion for him. He told him to get up and walk (verse 8).

When Jesus spoke, something began to happen. The man felt strength coming into his body. The legs that had been crippled these last thirty-eight years were filled with new strength and vitality. At once the man stood up, picked up his mat, and walked away. How overwhelmed he must have been to experience this miracle.

It is important to note that the day on which this miracle took place was the Sabbath. When the Jews saw the man carrying his mat on the Sabbath, they reminded him that the Law forbade the carrying of a burden on that day. Jeremiah the prophet made this clear: "This is what the LORD says: 'Be careful not to carry a load on the Sabbath day or bring it through the gates of Jerusalem'" (Jeremiah 17:21).

The man who had just been healed was in direct violation of the Law of Moses, according to the religious leaders. When questioned about why he was carrying his mat, the invalid told the religious leaders that the person who had healed him told him to pick up his mat and walk.

Why would Jesus invite someone to disobey the Law? Could Jesus not have waited a few more hours before healing this man? Could this man not have left his mat at the pool and come back for it when the Sabbath was over? Could he not have stayed a few more hours at the pool so that he would not be guilty of breaking the Sabbath law? To the Jews, Jesus was guilty of breaking the Sabbath. They would not forget this. This would not be the last time that they would accuse Jesus of breaking this law. This would become one of the major clashes between the Pharisees and Jesus. Jesus obviously did not have the same standard for the Sabbath as the Pharisees of his day. In Jesus' ministry, compassion and charity always overruled strict and unfeeling adherence to laws.

The Pharisees wanted the name of the person who had healed the disabled man. However, he did not know Jesus' name. He had been so excited about his healing that he had not noticed the healer. What a sad story this is. Here before us is a man who had been disabled for thirty-eight years. A perfect stranger came by and healed him. In his excitement he had not even taken the time to ask this stranger who he was and thank him.

What a great God we serve! Everything we have comes from his hand. Whether we are Christians or non-Christians, we owe this great God our lives, our possessions, and our families.

Jesus came to see the healed man at the temple (verse 14). Here Jesus reminded him of his sin. Jesus told the man to stop sinning so that something worse wouldn't happen to him. Those who have been touched by the Lord cannot casually continue in sin. It is important to note the warning of the Lord to the healed man. Jesus told him that if he continued to sin after having been touched by the Lord, something worse would happen to him. What could be worse than being crippled for thirty-eight years?

This is a challenge to us today. If the Lord has touched your life and you continue to live in sin, this passage is for you. Listen to what the apostle Peter tells us in this regard: "If they have escaped the corruption of the world by knowing our Lord and Savior Jesus Christ and are again entangled in it and overcome, they are worse off at the end than they were at the beginning. It would have been better for them not to have known the way of righteousness, than to have known it and then to turn their backs on the sacred command that was passed on to them" (2 Peter 2:20–21).

The challenge of this passage is real. If the Lord Jesus has touched our lives, we cannot go on living as we once did. We must surrender ourselves to him. Those who have been touched by Jesus experience a real change in their lives. They must turn from sin and seek him. This was a lesson the healed man needed to learn. It is also an important lesson for us as well.

For Consideration:

- In what way has the Lord Jesus touched your life? Give some examples of the things he has done for you.

- What has been your response to the things the Lord has done for you?

- Have you ever been guilty of the harsh observance of the Law and neglected to show compassion and love for those around you?

- What is the difference between knowing about the Lord Jesus and knowing him personally?

For Prayer:

- Thank the Lord for the many things he has done for you.

- Ask him to help you never to return to the old way of living now that he has touched you.

- Thank him for his great patience with you when you fall short of his standard.

12

Like Father, Like Son

Read John 5:16–30

The context is a discussion on the Sabbath. Jesus had healed a man who had been an invalid for thirty-eight years. The Jews had challenged him because he had healed this man on the Sabbath and encouraged him to carry his mat. To the Jews, this was in direct violation of the Law of Moses. In this section Jesus defended himself against the accusations of the Jews.

Jesus' defense was based on the fact that he did only what his heavenly Father would himself do. "My Father is always at his work to this very day, and I, too, am working" (verse 17). Jesus was reminding the Pharisees that God did not cease from his activities on the Sabbath. He continued to heal and provide.

This statement did not please the Jewish leaders. Though they could not argue with the fact that the Father never stopped working, they were severely offended at what Jesus was saying. To the Jew, Jesus was claiming equal authority with the Father. He was saying that because the Father worked, he too had the right to work on the Sabbath. This was blasphemous in the Jewish mind. God had the right to do as he pleased. People, however, were to be submissive to the Father and his Law. The Jews could not accept what Jesus was saying. They felt so strongly about this that they wanted to kill him (verse 18). Knowing their thoughts, Jesus explained to the Jews the relationship between his Father and himself. Let us examine Jesus' teaching on this.

Jesus began by telling the Pharisees that he could do nothing by himself (verse 19). He could only do what he saw the Father doing. Jesus was telling them that he never acted independently of the Father. The union between the Father and the Son was such that they were in perfect agreement with each other in all things. The Son only did what pleased the Father.

Next, Jesus explained that the Father loved the Son and showed him all that he did. The relationship between the Father and the Son was such that God the Father revealed to his Son all that he wanted to do. We have already seen an example of this in the healing of the man at the pool. Jesus did not heal the man because he thought it would be a good thing to do. He healed him because the Father had revealed to him that it was his desire to set this man free. There were others at the pool that day who were not healed. God the Father had revealed his purposes for this particular man to his Son, Jesus. The reason the Father revealed his heart to the Son was because he loved him and delighted to share his heart with him.

Is it not the delight of the Father to reveal his heart with us as well? If I listen carefully, he will lead and guide me too. I have often heard him prompting me. That prompting led me to the mission field. It also led me home to minister in my own hometown. This writing ministry is also a result of listening to the Father reveal his heart to me. Why should

God even care to reveal to me his heart? As in the case of his Son, it is out of love for me. What a privilege it is to have a God who loves me in this way.

Then Jesus told the Jews that the healing of the man at the pool was only one small example of the works that his Father delighted to do (verses 21–22). They would see even greater works than these. Jesus gave them two examples of these greater works.

First, he told them that just as the Father has the power to raise the dead and give life to whomever he desires, so he has given that same power to the Son. The Son of God too gives life to whomever he desires. The Son has the power of the Father to raise the dead. He has the power to give eternal life to whomever he pleases (verse 21).

Second, he told them that the Father has entrusted all judgment to the Son (verse 22). The destiny of humanity is in the hands of the Son. The Father accepts without question the judgment of the Son and condemns those whom the Son condemns. Those to whom the Son grants pardon and forgiveness are pardoned and forgiven by the Father.

We can only imagine the response of the Jews who stood before Jesus that day. They had been condemning him because they saw him as a breaker of the Sabbath law. Now Jesus was claiming that he was equal with God and that their destiny depended on him. This would not have been easy for the Jews to take.

He who honors the son honors the father (verse 23)

Jesus told the Jews that anyone who does not honor the Son does not honor the Father who sent him. There is such an intimate relationship between the Father and the Son that to dishonor one is to dishonor the other. All the glory we give the Father, we must also give to the Son. You cannot reject the Son and honor the Father. To turn your back on Christ is to turn your back on God the Father. The Father and the Son are united in the glory due to them. The Son is not less than the Father. All the glory that the Father receives, the Son is also worthy of receiving.

Verse 24 tells us that to hear and believe in the Lord Jesus is to have eternal life. This is the power the Father has given to him. We cannot take the Lord Jesus lightly. The day is coming when he will call out with a loud voice to the dead (verse 25). In the Father's name, the Lord Jesus has been given the authority to judge all men and women (verses 26–27). On that day of judgment, the dead will be raised from their graves. Those who have done good will be raised to life (verse 29). What does it mean to do good? The reward of those who do good is the resurrection of their bodies and eternal life with Christ (verse 29). Jesus already stated that only those who believe in him and hear his voice will receive this eternal life (verse 24). To do good, in this context, is to believe in the Lord Jesus Christ and to hear and obey his Word.

On the other hand, those who have done evil will be raised to condemnation (verse 29). To do good is to believe in the Lord Jesus and to obey his word. To do evil is to refuse the Lord Jesus and live as we please. While eternal life is the reward of the one who does good, eternal condemnation is the reward of the one who does evil. The judgment of the Lord Jesus is the judgment of the Father. They are in perfect harmony in this matter.

As he lived and moved on this earth, Jesus was in constant communion with his Father. If the Lord Jesus needed to be in constant communion with the Father, how much more should we? How much of what we do is based on our own understanding of what should be done? As Jesus served his Father, he willingly died to his own will. He yielded himself perfectly to the will of his Father. He sought to be in constant communion with God. He healed men and women as he sensed the direction and prompting of the Father. He spoke those things he sensed the Father placing on his heart. He will judge, even as the Father leads him to judge. There is perfect harmony between Jesus and the Father. We too must learn to know the Father in this way.

For Consideration:

- What do we learn here in this section about the relationship between the Lord Jesus and the Father?

- Are you hearing from the Lord? How does God lead us today? How important is it that we know his leading and direction? How important was it for the Lord Jesus?

- Has the Lord spoken to you about an area of your life where you are not listening to him? What is it in particular? What needs to be your response?

For Prayer:

- Ask God to forgive you for the times you have not taken the time to hear his voice.

- Thank the Lord Jesus for the fact that, though he is equal with the Father, he became man and lived among us.

- Thank the Lord for the fact that he still wants to lead and direct us as his children. Ask him to open your ears more and more to his leading.

13

The Five Witnesses

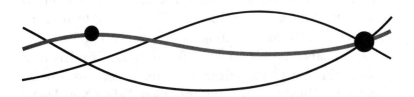

Read John 5:31–47

J esus had healed a man who had been disabled for thirty-eight years. Jesus had told him to pick up his mat on the Sabbath and carry it. The Pharisees accused Jesus of violating the law of the Sabbath. For the Jew, this was a crime punishable by death. In our last meditation, in defense of himself and his actions, Jesus told the Jews about his relationship with the Father. Here he called on five witnesses to support his defense before his Jewish accusers. According to the law of the time, the word of one person was not sufficient in a court of law (verse 31). A person needed to have a witness to validate testimony. Jesus would call on five witnesses to his character and deity.

The first witness to the character and deity of Christ was John the Baptist (verses 32–35). Jesus commended John for giving a true and faithful testimony (verse 32). What did John the Baptist say about the Lord Jesus? He told his followers that Jesus was the "Lamb of God, who takes away the sin of the world" (1:29). There can be no doubt as to the teaching of John the Baptist regarding the person of Christ. Jesus was the one who was to come from the Father to take away our sin.

John 5:35 tells us that for a time the Jews enjoyed hearing what John was preaching. He preached about the coming of the Messiah and challenged his listeners to prepare themselves for his coming. When the Jews met Jesus, however, they were disappointed. They had expected another type of Messiah. They had expected a political leader, not a meek spiritual leader. They turned their backs on him and rejected the testimony of John the Baptist.

Jesus called on his second witness (verse 36). His own work testified that he was from God. His miracles were proof that he was filled with the power of God. When Nicodemus came to Jesus, he recognized that Jesus was from God because of the miracles he had seen him do (3:2). While speaking to the Pharisees, Jesus challenged them to believe in him because of the works that he did: "But if I do it, even though you do not believe me, believe the miracles, that you may know and understand that the Father is in me, and I in the Father" (10:38). What else could explain the miraculous power of our Lord Jesus apart from the fact that God the Father was working in him? The Jews refused to believe these works. In spite of the evidence that surrounded them, they closed their eyes and blocked their ears. They refused to see the obvious.

Jesus next called on his third witness (verses 37–38). He called on the Father himself. What greater witness could there be? God the Father bore witness to the truth of the Son. When Jesus was baptized, the Father spoke in an audible voice to those who witnessed his baptism. "As soon as Jesus was baptized, he went up out of the water. At that moment heaven was opened, and he saw the Spirit of God descending like a dove and lighting on him. And a voice from heaven said, 'This is my Son, whom I love; with him I am well pleased'" (Matthew 3:16–17).

In John 1:32–34 we read that this incident was a definite sign from the Father that Jesus was the Son of God: "Then John gave this testimony: 'I saw the Spirit come down from heaven as a dove and remain on him. I would not have known him, except that the one who sent me to baptize with water told me, "The man on whom you see the Spirit come down and remain is he who will baptize with the Holy Spirit." I have seen and I testify that this is the Son of God.'"

The Father himself bore witness that Jesus was indeed his beloved Son. The Father's testimony alone, if you reject all the other witnesses, is sufficient to prove that Jesus is the Son of God, the Savior of the world. The Jews refused to listen even to the voice of God the Father. Does this not show us how hard the human heart can be? They would not listen to the Father because his Word did not dwell in them. They were lost in their sin and could not hear the voice of God.

Jesus called on his fourth witness (verses 39–40). He called on the Scriptures. The Jews highly regarded the Scriptures. You do not have to read very far in the Scriptures to discover that the central theme is Christ himself. Page after page points the sinner to the Savior. Jesus is the fulfillment of Scripture. The Jews carefully studied the Scriptures. They knew enough of the Scriptures to tell Jesus that he had broken the law of the Sabbath, but they had missed the central theme. The Jews turned their backs on the teaching of Scripture. They saw only what they wanted to see and ignored the rest. These Scriptures alone have convinced many people that Jesus is the Son of God. The Jews of Jesus' day, however, could not see this.

Before calling on his final witness, the Lord Jesus tells us something about the Jews in his day. He gives us two reasons why the Jewish leaders refused every witness to his deity. He tells us first, that the Jewish leaders, though they served God, did not have the love of God in their hearts (verse 42). They were religious because of the glory it would bring to them. They did not serve God because they loved him. Second, Jesus tells us that the Jews loved the praise of people rather that the praise of God (verses 41–44). The praise of people can quickly lead to our downfall. Many ministers of the gospel have fallen away from the truth of the Word of God because, like the Pharisees, they loved the praise of people. They were willing to compromise the truth to have others think more highly of them. The reason the Jewish leaders rejected all the witnesses to Christ was that they did not have the love of God in their hearts. They were committed to seeking the praise of people.

Finally, Jesus called on his last witness. He called on Moses himself (verses 45–47). The Jews had a deep admiration for Moses as their spiritual father. The reason they had accused Jesus of breaking the Sabbath was because of their respect for the Law of Moses. Jesus told them that when it came time for them to be judged, Moses would judge them himself. The very person they claimed to follow would find them guilty. Jesus reminded them that Moses believed in the Messiah. Moses would have bowed down in submission to him as the Messiah. The Jews did not accept the teachings of their own spiritual father. They had turned their backs on Moses.

You be the judge. Jesus has called on his witnesses. All five witnesses are unanimous. They all declare him to be the Son of God. Will we be like the Jews and turn our backs on him or will we accept the facts that are presented here?

For Consideration:

• What evidence is there today that Jesus is the Son of God? What evidence is there in your own life?

- Why do you suppose so many people reject the Lord Jesus?

- What blinds our eyes today to the things of God?

- What blinded your eyes to the Lord? What did it take for the Lord to make himself real to you?

For Prayer:

- Do you know some people who, like the Pharisees, have rejected the reality of Christ in their lives? Take a moment to pray that the Lord would reveal himself to them in a way they cannot deny.

- Thank him that he revealed himself to you.

- Thank the Lord Jesus that, as the Son of God, he willingly came to this earth to die for our sin.

14

The Feeding of the Five Thousand

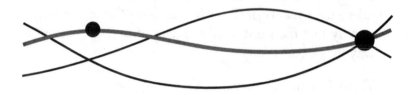

Read John 6:1–15

Some time had passed since his last encounter with the Pharisees in Jerusalem. Jesus was now on the far side of the Sea of Galilee. A large crowd had gathered around him and his disciples. The crowd was following Jesus because they had seen his miracles. Those who followed Jesus that day were not true believers. They were interested more in his miracles than they were in him as the Savior.

Possibly weary of this type of follower, the Lord Jesus decided to go to the mountain with his disciples. Verse 3 leads us to believe that he did not take the crowd with him. This was a private moment with his disciples. He sat down with them on the mountainside. We are not told what they did on that mountain. Maybe the Lord spent time teaching them and preparing them for what was about to happen. What is sure here is that they needed to get away from the crowd and spend time together. This is no less important today. How important it is for us, as well, to take time to get away from the pressing crowd to spend time alone with the Lord.

From verse 4 we learn that the Jewish Passover was near. Why does John feel compelled to tell us this? It is quite likely that the large crowd that had been following Jesus that day had come for the celebration of the Passover. If this is the case, this crowd was likely composed of Jews from many different places.

The crowd found Jesus on the mountainside. When he saw the crowd, Jesus felt compassion for them (verse 5). He knew that they had been some time without food. He turned to Philip to ask him where they could buy bread for this crowd to eat.

The response of Philip is understandable: "Eight months' wages would not buy enough bread for each one to have a bite!" (verse 7). Where would the disciples get this sort of money? They had left everything to follow the Lord. Philip did not understand what the Lord was trying to say. We learn from verse 6 that Jesus said this to Philip to test him. There have been times when the Lord has tested me in a similar way. Maybe you too have been tested like this in your life. The Lord will sometimes place us before an impossible situation to see if we will turn to him for the solution.

Andrew must have overheard Jesus' conversation with Philip. He approached Jesus to tell him that there was a little boy present with five loaves of bread and two fishes. That is all they could find. Had he inquired among the people to see if anyone had brought food? If enough people had brought food, they could share that food with the others. Maybe there would be enough for each person to have a small bite. His search revealed nothing but these five loaves and two fishes. What was this compared to the number of people who needed to be fed?

It is interesting to see the response of these two disciples. When Jesus asked them where they would get enough food to feed the crowd, they looked to themselves. Philip looked at how much money they had. Andrew looked to the people around him. Neither one of these men looked to the Lord. How easy it is to fall into the same trap. Jesus was the only one who could provide the answer to this problem, but no one thought to look to him or ask him.

Jesus had the people sit on the grass. The Bible tells us that there were five thousand men present. We also know that there was a least one little boy because he gave his lunch to the Lord Jesus. It is quite likely that there were also many other children as well as many women present. When this large crowd was seated, the Lord took the five loaves and two fishes, broke them, and gave them to the disciples to distribute to the crowd.

We are not told how this miracle took place. I am assuming that when the Lord handed them the basket to distribute among the crowd, it contained only what he had put in it of the five loaves and two fishes. The food seemed to multiply as it was passed from person to person.

Verse 11 is important for us to note. The Bible tells us that each person took as much bread and fish as they wanted. This is not something you do when you know that there is a short supply of food. Jesus, however, encouraged them to take all they wanted. They were not to worry about whether the person next to them would have any. There would be no shortage. When it comes to the provision of the heavenly Father, you never need to fear that you will not have enough. God's grace is limitless. You can never exhaust his supplies.

There are times when we hesitate to come to the Lord. We are afraid of bringing our requests to him. It is as though we do not want to bother him with our small requests. We sometimes pray as though God's grace were being rationed, as though only the most urgent requests will be granted. This verse challenges us to bring every request to the Lord. Do not think that you can ever exhaust his supply of grace. He has enough grace for your every request and plenty left over for the rest of the world too. Come boldly to him in prayer. Do not hesitate to reach your hand into the basket and take as much as your heart desires. If you go hungry, it is not because of a shortage of bread—it is because you did not take what the Lord was offering you.

The Bible tells us that every person present had all they wanted to eat. As if to emphasize that there was no limit to the grace of God, Jesus asked his disciples to gather up what remained. Notice that there was more left over than when they started! This teaches us something else about the grace of God. The more you take, the more it multiplies.

What was the response of the people to this miracle? They understood that Jesus was no ordinary person. They believed him to be the prophet who was to come (verse 14). They wanted to make him king. What a king he would be. Here was a king who could guarantee no more hunger. Here was a king who could guarantee no more sickness and disease. This was the sort of king they wanted. He would fix all their problems.

The time is coming when Jesus will reign as king in a kingdom where there will be no more hunger, sickness, or dying. This, however, was not the time. Jesus decided to leave the crowd. He went up onto a mountain to spend some time alone with his Father. It must have hurt him to see the reaction of the crowd. They were only thinking about themselves and how they could profit from having Jesus as their king.

The wonderful thing about the Lord Jesus is that you can come to him with all of your problems. As a God of compassion and mercy, he is able and willing to heal you of your hurts and minister to your needs. Remember, however, that though he is full of grace and compassion, he is not some object to be used like a magic wand or magic potion to cater to your every whim. This was how the crowd saw him. Jesus would have nothing to do with this. What an injustice the crowd did to our Lord that day. They cared nothing for him. They cared only for what they could get out of him. For this reason the Lord left them.

For Consideration:

- Do you have time alone with the Lord? Why is this time important to you?

- Do you find yourself looking to others for help when you should be looking to Jesus? What do you depend on in your times of trouble?

- Why is it so hard for us to draw deeply from the basket of the Lord's grace? Why are we content as Christians with so little?

- What was the crowd in Jesus' day seeking? Why do you think that the Lord Jesus turned from them?

For Prayer:

- Ask the Lord to forgive you for the times you did not look to him for help.

- Ask him to increase your faith and trust in him. Thank him for the times he puts you in impossible situations to show you his grace and provision.

- Is there a particular situation in your life that needs to be placed in the Lord's hands? Take a moment right now to give this matter over to the Lord.

- Thank the Lord that he is able and delights to provide.

15

The Miracle on the Lake

Read John 6:16–21

J esus had fed over five thousand people with five loaves and two small fish. The crowd responded by trying to make him king by force. Jesus withdrew into the mountains by himself. The disciples likely spent the rest of the day with the crowd. When it was evening, the disciples crossed the lake to the region of Capernaum. They left without Jesus. They did not realize how much they needed the Lord as they left that evening for what should have been a routine crossing of the lake.

It was late in the day when the disciples began their journey across the lake. As they set out on the lake, a great storm came up. The waters grew rough. Mark 6:48 tells us that the disciples were "straining at the oars, because the wind was against them." The storm made rowing very difficult. The disciples were in the middle of the lake. They couldn't turn back. It was getting darker by the minute, and soon they would not be able to see where they were going. They had had a full day with the feeding of the five thousand. They were tired. John tells us that they had already rowed about three miles (five or six kilometers) in this storm. Maybe, like the disciples, you have also grown weary. You really don't know what your future holds. You seem to be straining at the oars, just to get through each day. Maybe part of the problem is that you too, like the disciples, have left Jesus behind. Now you find yourself trying to get through this mess in your own strength but not succeeding. Maybe you can identify with the disciples on the lake.

It was at this point that these tired and weary disciples looked up into the storm and saw a figure approaching them on the water. They could not make out what it was. They were terrified. Mark tells us that they thought it was a ghost (Mark 6:49). The appearance of this figure only seemed to complicate things for the disciples at this point.

Sensing their fear, the Lord Jesus called out to them: "It is I; don't be afraid" (verse 20). What a relief it was to the disciples to hear the voice of the Lord. Though they were greatly astonished to see him walking on the water, they very gladly received him aboard their vessel.

According to Mark 6:48, Jesus met the disciples on the lake at the fourth watch of the night. This would have been about three o'clock in the morning. We have no way of telling how long the disciples had been struggling against that storm. It would appear that they had been fighting it for some time. They had rowed about three miles on the lake when the Lord met them. By three o'clock in the morning, they would certainly have been glad to see him. No wonder verse 21 tells us that they "were willing to take him into the boat."

When they invited Jesus into their boat, their struggle ended. They arrived immediately at their desired location. This was nothing short of a miracle. There are many people like the disciples on the sea of life. They are without the

Lord. A storm is raging in their souls. They know where they want to go. They want to get to heaven, but they are getting nowhere. They are fighting too many obstacles. They are fighting the waves and wind in the dark, not able to see their destination. They are growing weary. Any time now the storm will take their craft to the bottom of the lake, where they will perish forever.

Do you feel like the disciples? Do you feel like you are going in circles in your spiritual life with no direction? Do you feel like you are straining at the oars and getting nowhere spiritually? Could it be that the solution to your problem is the same as the solution the disciples discovered? Could it be that you have left the Lord behind? How easy it is for the enemy to deceive us into thinking that we can live the Christian life in our own strength. We busy ourselves with Christian activity. We fill up our schedules by doing good things. We strain at the oars but find ourselves weary and dry. Even as Christians we can strain at the oars. All too many Christians are trying to live the Christian life by themselves. Just as we must invite the Lord Jesus into our hearts for salvation so we must invite him to live the Christian life through us.

When the disciples invited the Lord into the boat, their wrestling ceased. The Lord Jesus gave them victory over the storm. Jesus was the answer to the disciples' problem. I am sure that he is the answer to your problem as well.

For Consideration:

- How much of your Christian life has been lived in your own strength? What does this passage teach you about your need of the Lord Jesus?

- Why is it so hard for us to admit that in our own strength we cannot live the life God requires?

- What is the difference between trying to live the Christian life in our own strength and letting the Lord live that life through us?

For Prayer:

- Ask the Lord to help you to understand what it means to allow him to take control of your life.

- Thank him that despite the fact that you have often left him behind, he has often come to your rescue.

- Thank him that he delights in reaching out to you in your difficulty.

16

Drawn by the Father

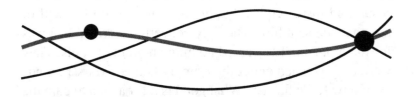

Read John 6:22–45

The disciples had just miraculously crossed the lake after the feeding of the five thousand. The crowd had remained there for the night. The next morning, when the people could not find Jesus, they set off in search of him. Finding some boats nearby, they left for the other side of the lake.

The crowd was somewhat confused when they found him on the other side of the lake. They knew that he had not crossed over in the boat with the disciples. How had he crossed the lake in the storm? They questioned him about this, but Jesus seemed to avoid their question. He knew exactly what they wanted. The day before they had wanted to make him king. With him as their king, the crowd believed that they would never be in need.

Jesus performed his miracles to help the people see that he was the Son of God. These miracles should have caused them to bow the knee before God's Anointed One. Seeing the power of the Lord, however, the people immediately began to think of how they could harness his power and use it for their own ends. They sought Jesus because he filled their bellies, not because he proved to them he was the Son of God. Why do people seek Jesus today? It is wonderful to see the power of God being demonstrated through signs and wonders. These signs, however, are not an end in themselves. They should draw us into a deeper walk with the Lord.

Knowing the mind of the crowd, Jesus challenged them to work for the food that lasted for eternity. In John 4:34 Jesus told his disciples that his food was to do the will of the one who sent him. The only concern the crowd had was for the moment. They cared nothing about their souls. They were only worried about their empty bellies. Mark reminds us of how futile this is: "What good is it for a man to gain the whole world, yet forfeit his soul?" (Mark 8:36).

Jesus challenged the crowd to take their eyes off their bellies for a moment and look at their souls. What would it profit them if they filled their bellies and lost their souls? All their efforts and thoughts centered on their present physical needs. Their bellies were filled, but their hearts were empty. "Do not work for food that spoils, but for food endures to eternal life" (verse 27). Jesus went on to tell them that he alone could give them this bread because the Father had set his seal of approval on him. The bread that Jesus was speaking about here was not physical bread that would satisfy the hunger of their bellies. He was referring to the salvation he came to offer that would bring them eternal life and satisfy their spiritual hunger forever.

The crowd did not understand what Jesus was telling them here. "What must we do to do the works God requires," they asked (verse 28).

"The work of God is this: to believe in the one he has sent," was Jesus' reply. This is all the work that God requires of someone who wants to obtain this bread he offers. Believe in the Lord Jesus Christ and he will fill every void and satisfy every longing of the human heart. There is nothing complicated about salvation. Believe and you will be saved. Believe and your destiny is assured. Believe and you are set free from the wrath of God. Believe and you become a child of God. Believe and your soul will be satisfied.

The crowd was not convinced about what the Lord was telling them. They felt that there needed to be something more than this. "What miraculous sign then will you give that we may see it and believe you," they asked Jesus (verse 30). As if to suggest a possible miracle, the people reminded Jesus of how their forefathers ate manna in the wilderness. In reality they were asking him to give them manna so that they could fill their bellies. Were they not proving, by this statement, what Jesus had been saying all along? They were only concerned about their physical needs. They were, in effect, saying: "Feed us and we will follow you."

Again Jesus sought to turn their eyes from the physical to the spiritual realm. He told them that the bread he had to offer was not like the bread that Moses gave his people in the wilderness. "For the bread of God is he who comes down from heaven and gives life to the world," Jesus told them (verse 33). Jesus spoke of himself as that bread that gives life to the world. He came so that our spiritual hunger could be satisfied. He came to give us life.

"From now on give us this bread," said the crowd (verse 34). They still did not understand what Jesus was saying. Whatever he was offering, however, they were willing to take.

"I am the bread," said Jesus (verse 35). "He who comes to me will never go hungry, and he who believes in me will never be thirsty." Jesus had told the Samaritan woman the same thing: "Everyone who drinks this water will be thirsty again, but whoever drinks the water I give him will never thirst. Indeed, the water I give him will become in him a spring of water welling up to eternal life" (4:13–14).

What a promise the Lord Jesus was making to the crowd that day. He offered them complete satisfaction for their souls. He offered them life eternal. The Lord Jesus is offering the same thing now. All that is required is that we believe what he says and take him at his word.

The sad thing about this story is that the Jews could not believe. Though they had seen the Lord Jesus with their very own eyes and heard his message, they did not believe what he was telling them. The miracles he performed were not enough for them. They were still blind to the Lord and his salvation. They could not understand, even though the facts were there in front of them.

As he looked at the Jews in their unbelief, Jesus reminded them that it was the will of the Father that everyone who looked to him and believed in his name would have eternal life (verse 40). If they came to him, he would never drive them away (verse 37). He would keep them to the end (verse 39). In spite of these excellent promises, the Jews turned their backs on the Lord. They could not accept his claim to being the bread from heaven (verse 41). They knew his parents (verse 42). They had seen him grow up. They could not accept his teaching.

Why could the Jews not believe in the Lord Jesus? With all the evidence they had, was it not obvious that he was who he claimed to be? Jesus tells us why they could not believe. He tells us in verse 44 that the only way that they could come to him was if the Father drew them. In verse 45 Jesus tells us that it is only those who hear the Father and are taught by him who will come to him. Jesus is telling us that if you and I are ever going to come to him and be saved, three things need to happen. First, we need to hear the voice of the Father. Second, we need the Father to teach us. Third, we need the Father to draw us to Christ.

Who among us can say that they came to the Lord on their own? Left to ourselves we would have continued in our sin. It was not until the Holy Spirit of God spoke to us, caused us to understand the truth of the Word, and drew us to the Lord Jesus that we understood the claims of Christ and accepted him as Lord and Savior. Our salvation is all of God. Were it not for the Father touching us by his Holy Spirit, teaching us his purpose and drawing us, we would still be in darkness today. The problem with the Jews that day was that they had not experienced this touch of God.

The task of converting souls does not belong to mankind. No amount of human reason will ever convince sinners to turn their lives over to the Lord Jesus. People in their natural, sinful state cannot understand the things of God nor do they want to accept them. Unless the Spirit of God touches the individual concerned, all our efforts will be fruitless. Only God can save a soul.

What does all this teach us? It teaches us that the first thing we need to do as we seek to reach our friends and neighbors for the gospel is to get down on our knees and pray. God will work in us and through us to cause them to understand. Though we are the instruments, it is only by his power alone that they can be drawn to the Lord Jesus. How we need to thank him today that he touched our lives and drew us to himself. If it were not for him, we would still be like the Jews of Jesus day—living in unbelief.

For Consideration:

- Jesus speaks of himself here as a bread that gives life. What does he mean by this?

- What do we learn here about the role of God in our salvation?

- Think back for a moment to the day of your conversion experience. What evidence is there of the Father drawing you to himself?

For Prayer:

- Thank the Lord for the gift of salvation.

- Confess your sins to the Lord and reach out in faith to his gift of salvation.

- Do you know someone who, like the Jews of Jesus' day, cannot see the Lord for who he really is? Take a moment to pray that the Lord would give this person eyes to see the truth.

17

The Bread of Life

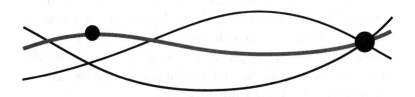

Read John 6:46–71

Jesus had been speaking with the crowd that had followed him to the other side of the lake. He told them that he was the bread which had come down from heaven. This was not the type of bread they were looking for. They had expected another type of Messiah. This teaching of the Lord Jesus about being the bread of life caused many difficulties for the crowd. In this section we will look at what Jesus had to say about the bread of life.

Jesus began his teaching on the bread of life by stating that whoever eats of this bread would have everlasting life. Jesus made it quite clear that he himself is the bread of life (verse 48). What Jesus was saying here was that if you want eternal life you must eat of him. This merits careful consideration. What does it mean to eat of Christ? From verse 52 we see that the Jews had a real problem understanding what Jesus was telling them. "How can this man give us his esh to eat?" they asked (verse 52). There are a few things that will help us to understand what Jesus meant by this statement.

First, when we eat our food, we become one with our food. The food we eat is taken into our bodies and broken down to regenerate and build up our bodies. In other words, the phrase "you are what you eat" is literally true. As the process of digestion takes place and the food breaks down, eventually this food works its way into every tissue and fiber of our being. What Jesus is telling us is that this is what he wants to be in us. He doesn't want to be someone we think about only on Sunday at church or when we get into trouble. He wants to become part of every cell and fiber in us. He wants to be part of every decision, goal, or ambition in life. He wants to become so much a part of us that we can no longer distinguish him from ourselves.

Second, the food we eat is our source of life and energy. Without that food we would perish. Our very life depends on this food. I believe Jesus is calling us to come to the realization here that without him we can do nothing. We are absolutely dependent on him for our life and breath. He calls us to draw our strength, wisdom, and energy from him. Jesus is telling us here that he wants to be our life and strength in everything we do. What a privilege this is.

While it is true that we must eat to live, eating is one of the few things we do to survive that gives us great pleasure. Eating is not a boring ritual. Eating is one of life's most pleasant experiences. So pleasant is the experience that we often invite others to participate with us in it. There is nothing more wonderful in life than feasting on the Lord Jesus. He is the source of tremendous joy and happiness. In him is fulfillment and satisfaction beyond measure. We can experience this by seeking him and eating of him.

When Jesus tells us that we must eat his esh, he is speaking symbolically. He is inviting us to participate in one of life's most pleasant experiences. It is an experience that you will want to share with others. He is inviting us to make him part of our lives and thoughts. He is inviting us to accept him and allow him to enter our lives to cleanse and strengthen. He alone can satisfy and fill our souls to over owing.

Having said this, we must now return to what Jesus is telling us here about feasting on him. He tells us in this section that those who feast on him will have everlasting life. Jesus repeated this five times in this short section of Scripture. (See verses 50, 51, 54, 57, 58.) Obviously, Jesus was trying to drive this point home to the crowd. Jesus was making an important statement here. He is telling us that the only way to have eternal life is to eat the bread of life. This bread alone is able to give us eternal life. It does not matter how many good things we have done in this life or how many times a week we go to church. If we have not eaten of the bread of life (the Lord Jesus) we will perish in our sins. When we stand before the gates of heaven, the only thing that God is going to look for is whether or not the Lord Jesus is in us. He alone is our guarantee of eternal life.

We all know what it is like to be hungry. We have also experienced the difference that eating a good meal makes to a hungry body. In a similar way, when we accept the Lord Jesus into our heart, we too will experience a very definite sense of new life in us. Christ will bring a very radical change to our life. We will know his power and his presence owing through us. His strength becomes our strength and his desires, our desires. Our goals are his goals. Our ambitions are his ambitions. We are one in purpose, effort, and will.

The promise of the Lord Jesus to those who have his life in them is that he will raise them up on the last day (verse 54). Again notice the condition attached to this promise. You must eat of the Lord Jesus. He must be part of you. His life must be owing through you. The promise of being raised up to glory in the last day is not for everyone. Only those who have Christ's life in them can know this eternal life and be raised up on that day.

What Jesus offers here is as real as any physical food could ever be. He tells us that his flesh is real food. We should not see this in the physical sense. What Jesus is telling us is that his flesh is spiritual food, but it is as real as any food we will ever eat here below. There is a real satisfaction that comes from eating of this bread of life. There is real spiritual life that is offered to all who will eat. There is a real eternity that is being prepared for those who have tasted the bread of life. This is not a fanciful story or some unreal ideal. This is life itself. What Jesus offers us in his own body is as real as the physical reality around us.

One of the things about eating the bread of life is that it has permanent effects on our lives. Before eating of the bread of life, realize that the decision you are about to make has permanent implications. When you eat of this bread, you are surrendering yourself completely to the Lord Jesus. Once you have eaten your physical food, it will be digested by your body and become part of who you are. This is the way it is with the bread of life. Once you have accepted the Lord Jesus into your life, there is no turning back. The decision you make to allow him into your heart is a "forever" decision. Jesus said: "Whoever eats my flesh and drinks my blood remains in me, and I in him" (verse 56). He comes to stay. There will be no turning back once you eat of the bread of life. You will be forever changed.

As Christ drew his life from the Father, he offers that same life to everyone today (verse 57). We live because he has life and is the author of life. That life is eternal. He offers this to all who will yield completely to him today.

What was the response of those who followed Jesus that day? What Jesus said was offensive to some. They questioned how Jesus could make such claims. Knowing their thoughts,

Jesus prophesied that the day was coming when they would see him ascending up into heaven, returning to his Father (verse 62). He also assured them that the words he spoke were from the Spirit and they contained life. These words were no ordinary words; they were empowered by God and contained the secret of eternal life. The people who listened to Jesus that day could not see the power of these words because the Spirit of God was not in them. Only those who had the Spirit of God in them could understand and accept the words Jesus spoke. Unless the Father drew them and gave them understanding, these people could never accept his words (verse 65).

After hearing what Jesus said, many in the crowd left Jesus, never to return. This did not surprise Jesus. You can be a follower of Christ and not a true believer. These people followed Jesus wherever he went. They heard him preach and saw his miracles. They were clearly associated with the Lord Jesus, but they had never eaten the bread of life. Jesus had not become their life. They knew nothing about Jesus living in them. When Jesus saw the crowd leave that day, he turned to his twelve disciples and asked them if they too were going to leave. They responded: "We believe and know that you are the Holy One of God" (verse 69). Jesus knew, however, that even among the twelve that followed him, there was one who was not a true believer. Judas would one day betray him. Among the closest followers of Jesus was one who had never eaten of the bread of life.

Being a Christian is more than a set of rules and regulations. It is more than church and a Bible. Being a Christian is having the very God of the universe come to live in your soul. It is having the life of God ow through your veins. It is experiencing the power and the presence of Christ in our life, transforming our heart and our will.

For Consideration:

• What does it mean to eat of the bread of life?

• Have you eaten of the bread of life? What evidence is there of this new life in you today?

• What is the difference between being a "follower" of Christ and a person who has eaten of the bread of life?

For Prayer:

• Thank the Lord for the evidence of his life in you.

• If you do not know this life of Christ in you today, take a moment to ask him to reveal the truth of this passage to you.

• Do you know someone who is only a "follower" of Christ? Take a moment to pray that God would reveal himself to this person in a clearer way.

18

Who is Jesus? (Part 1)

Read John 7:1–24

Who is Jesus? This has been one of the world's most debated questions. It was debated among Jewish leaders in the days that Christ walked on the earth. Pilate asked the question in his own heart before he crucified our Lord. The apostles answered this question many times throughout their ministry. In our day the discussion continues. In theological seminaries and universities throughout our nations, the question of who Jesus is, is still being debated. In the next two meditations we will examine the ideas of the people of Jesus' day concerning his identity.

The time for the Jewish Feast of Tabernacles was approaching. Jesus had been staying away from the region of Judea because the Jews there were seeking to kill him. With the approach of the Jewish Feast of Tabernacles, Jesus left Galilee and made the journey to Judea.

As they prepared for the feast, Jesus' brothers came to

him with a recommendation. They told Jesus that this feast would be the ideal time for him to make a big name for himself. People would be gathering from many parts of the Jewish world in Jerusalem. It would be the ideal time for him to show his power and gain a larger following. "No man who wants to become a public figure acts in secret," they told him (verse 4).

We can only wonder what the brothers of Jesus thought of him and his ministry. Verse 5 tells us that they did not believe in him. Are you the only Christian in your family? Jesus knows what it is like not to have the spiritual support of family members. His brothers saw Jesus as a public figure. They saw him as a promoter of new truth. They saw him as a person who did good works. They saw him as a miracle worker. While his brothers had respect for what the Lord was doing, they did not believe he was the Son of God.

This attitude has continued till today. There are many people who see the Lord Jesus in this light. They see him as a "doer of good deeds." They see him as a great teacher. They see him as a man whose teaching needs to be respected. This, however, is as far as they are willing to go. To these people, Christianity is a philosophy of life. It is a lifestyle. They respect the teachings and example of Jesus and see these as very commendable. They follow him because they believe in his ideals.

When his brothers brought up the issue of the Lord Jesus going to Jerusalem to make a name for himself, Jesus reminded them of the hatred of the Jews toward him (verses 6–7). His brothers could go to Jerusalem with no fear. They were not hated. As for Jesus, however, he preached against the hypocrisy he saw around him. He spoke out against the evil of his day. The Jews hated him because of what he said about them. They hated him because he threatened their reputations. They wanted to kill him. Jesus encouraged his brothers to go to Jerusalem without him. It was not time for him to go.

Jesus was not interested in seeking the type of followers that his brothers thought he should have. He knew that he could do a few miracles and there would be a following of people behind him. These people, however, would abandon him the moment he spoke to them about their sin. How easy it is in our day to be interested in a Jesus who protects, comforts, and heals but not in a Jesus who calls us to self-denial and death to self. Jesus would remind his disciples later in his ministry that those who wanted to follow him would first have to pick up their cross. He told them that there was no other way to follow him. This type of Jesus was harder to accept.

Jesus went to Jerusalem in secret. The Jews were looking for him. The crowd too was looking for Jesus. There was great division over who he was. Some people in Jerusalem felt, like the brothers of Jesus, that he was a good man, whose teaching was to be respected (verse 12). His miracles had shown them that he was walking close to God. Others totally rejected him.

Those who rejected him went as far as to say that he was a deceiver. They had heard his teaching. They had seen his miracles. They believed, however, that our Lord was an impostor. They refused to attribute his miracles to the power of God. They refused to accept his teaching. For them, Jesus was deceiving people for his own ends.

In our day the media has reported cases of religious leaders who have been uncovered as deceivers. They came in the name of truth. They came with the power to do signs and wonders. They were men and women of incredible ability and authority. They succeeded in gathering large followings of people, but they were deceivers. This was how the Jews saw our Lord.

Halfway through the feast, the Lord Jesus began to

teach in the temple. When the Jews heard him, they were astonished at his knowledge. They wondered how it was that a man with no formal theological and biblical education could know so much. To this question the Lord answered: "My teaching is not my own. It comes from him who sent me" (verse 16). Jesus went on to tell his listeners that the only way they could be assured that what he was teaching was the truth was if they themselves were living in the will of God (verse 17). Anyone with an open mind who sought to do the will of the Father would know that Jesus was teaching the truth. If you do not know the truth, you cannot judge it. If you have never experienced the truth of God in your own life, how can you say that those who have are misled? This was a real slap in the face to the Pharisees. Jesus was telling them that they had never experienced the truth. Because they were living in error, they had no way of judging whether what he was saying was true.

Possibly thinking about what his brothers had told him (verse 4), Jesus reminded the leaders that he did not come to seek the praise of men but to do the will of the Father (verse 18). There were those who had been accusing him of seeking a following for his own glory. Was Jesus a man obsessed with his own glory and honor? Was he a man who lived his life in search of the praise of men? There were some who felt that this was his motivation. A simple look at the life of our Lord, however, would prove these people wrong. In all of Scripture we never see Jesus thinking of himself. He is always ministering to others. He healed and cast out demons reminding people not to tell others of what he had done. When people came to make him king, he departed from them. When his brothers told him that he needed to do more of his works in public to be seen by the people, he refused to listen to them. Satan one day told our Lord that if he would only bow down to him, he would give him the kingdoms of the world—Jesus refused.

Jesus knew that the Pharisees were angry with him because he had healed a man on the Sabbath. (See John 5.) They saw him as a lawbreaker. They were trying to cast doubt on his ministry. Jesus challenged them on this issue. He reminded them of how they were willing to circumcise a man on the Sabbath but refused to allow physical healing. He challenged them with this lack of compassion. Because he had displayed compassion on the Sabbath toward a man who had been an invalid for thirty-eight years, they sought to kill him. Jesus showed them their hypocrisy. They were more concerned for their traditions than they were for people. They claimed he did wrong because he healed a man on the Sabbath but had no problem committing murder to get rid of Jesus. There was a sad inconsistency here.

What Jesus told the Pharisees cut them deeply. They accused him of being demon-possessed (verse 20). To the Pharisee, Jesus was proposing another religion. He was an enemy of their customs and religious practices. They hated him and what he stood for. They accused him of being a Satan-inspired and demon-possessed radical who sought to break down everything that had been handed down to them from their spiritual forefathers.

What did the people in Jesus' day think about him? We have seen at least four different proposals in this section of Scripture.

1. He was a good teacher or philosopher offering a new way of life.
2. He was a religious deceiver.
3. He was a seeker of praise.
4. He was a demon-inspired radical, seeking to destroy the organized religion of the day.

How it hurts those of us who have accepted the Lord Jesus as the Son of God to see these responses to our Savior.

I assure you that the Lord Jesus is none of the above. The apostle John, as he wrote this book, was aware of the confusion regarding the identity of Jesus. His purpose in writing his Gospel was to clear up this confusion: "But these are written that you may believe that Jesus is the Christ, the Son of God, and that by believing you may have life in his name" (20:31).

For Consideration:

- What opinions have you heard about the Lord Jesus in our day?

- Why is it so hard for people to accept the Lord Jesus as the Son of God?

- Is there evidence in your church of people who want the comfort and security of knowing Jesus but do not want to hear him speak to them about their sin?

- What is the difference between the traditions of our churches and the Lord Jesus? Have you ever found yourself seeking after these externals more than seeking the Lord?

For Prayer:

- If you are not sure of what you think about the Lord Jesus today, ask God to reveal him to you over the course of the next few meditations in this book.

- Is there someone among your acquaintances who does not know the Lord Jesus as the Son of God? Pray that God would reveal himself to this person.

- If you know the Lord Jesus today, thank him that he has made himself known to you.

19

Who is Jesus?
(Part 2)

Read John 7:25–53

The debate over the identity of Jesus continued. Jesus was speaking here with the Pharisees, as the crowd looked on. The crowd did not understand why their spiritual leaders, who wanted to kill Jesus, now spoke so freely with him. Some even wondered if the Pharisees had come to accept him as the Christ. One of the problems for the crowd was that they knew where Jesus was born. They could not imagine that he could be any different from them, because they knew his family and his hometown. Some had seen Jesus grow up. To them this was proof that Jesus had not come from God.

Knowing their thoughts, Jesus reminded them that while he was born among them, he was sent from above (verses 28–29). He reminded them that they could not recognize him as the Messiah because they did not know the One who sent him. This statement angered the crowd. They tried to seize him. They were insulted by what he was saying to them. They considered themselves to be religious people who served God. Jesus was telling them that they were only fooling themselves. The crowd could not harm Jesus, however, "because his time had not yet come" (verse 30). What a wonderful hope we have here. There is nothing that people can do to us that interferes with God's plan for us. God protects us until our mission has been accomplished. We can step out in all boldness because God is with us and will enable us to accomplish that purpose for which he has called us.

Among the crowd that day were certain individuals who did believe that Jesus was the Son of God (verse 30). The miracles they had seen Jesus do were proof enough for them that he was the Christ. Knowing that certain people among the crowd were being persuaded by the teaching and works of Jesus, the chief priests and Pharisees sent temple guards to arrest him (verse 32).

In verse 34 Jesus told the crowd that he would only be with them a short while. He told them that he would leave them and go to a place where they would not be able to find him. Jesus was referring here to his death and ascension to the Father. The Jews present that day did not understand. Some thought he was going to leave them and go to another place to teach (verses 35–36).

The temple guards, who had been sent to arrest Jesus, followed him, waiting for the ideal moment to seize him. As they followed they heard him speak to the crowds. The guards listened intently to what Jesus was saying. While they very likely were listening with the intention of finding fault with his teaching and an occasion to arrest him, they witnessed his effect on people.

On one occasion, the Lord told the crowd that if anyone was thirsty, they could come to him and drink (verse 37). He told them that if they believed in him, rivers of living water would ow within them. These living waters would forever quench their spiritual thirst. John tells us that Jesus was referring to the Holy Spirit when he spoke about this living water (verse 39).

The crowd was touched by these words. Some believed Jesus to be a real prophet from God. Other said that he was much more than a prophet—he was Messiah, the Christ (verse 41). Still others remained hardened and wanted to seize him. As for the temple guards sent to arrest Jesus, what they heard the Lord say touched them as well. Verse 45 tells us that they returned empty-handed to the chief priests and Pharisees. "Why didn't you bring him in?" the leaders inquired (verse 45). "No one ever spoke the way this man does" was the reply (verse 46).

The temple guards had been sent out to arrest the Lord Jesus. As they listened to what he taught, however, they were so touched that they could not lay a hand on him. So powerful were the words of Christ that they chose to disobey their superiors and suffer the consequences rather than touch the Lord Jesus and be guilty before God.

In their pride, the Pharisees reminded the temple guards that it was only the ignorant masses of people who believed in Jesus (verses 48–49). They, however, as the teachers of the Law, had not been deceived. As they spoke to the guards, Nicodemus interrupted them. Nicodemus, like the temple guards, had taken the time to listen to Jesus. (See John 3.) He spoke to his fellow Pharisees. He told them that they would be wise not to judge Jesus until they had first examined what he preached and what he had been doing. To this they replied: "Are you from Galilee, too?" (verse 52). In saying this they were insulting him. To them nothing of any value could come from Galilee. The Pharisees judged Jesus on the basis of where he was from and not on the basis of his teaching and evidence of his anointing. They closed their minds to anything they did not want to hear.

The advice of Nicodemus is very good advice for us today. Don't turn your backs on the Lord Jesus until you have carefully examined his claims. Don't reject him until you have looked at his works. Among the crowd that day were a few people who had opened their eyes and ears and examined the facts. They came to the conclusion that Jesus was all he said he was.

The temple guards, some of the crowd, and Nicodemus, having taken the time to hear his claims and see his works, recognized and confessed Jesus to be the Christ, the Son of God. As for the Pharisees and the rest of the crowd, they blocked their ears. They closed their eyes to his miracles. They chose to listen to their traditions and the voice of their own sinful hearts.

What about you? Who is Jesus? If you want to answer this question, you must open your ears and eyes to hear and see the evidence around you. Don't be like the Pharisees. Open your heart and mind. Let the Word of God speak to you. Let the Holy Spirit convince you. Look at the evidence that is presented to you. Only then will you be able to answer this most important question.

For Consideration:

- What kept the Pharisees from listening to the claims of the Lord Jesus?

- Why do you suppose the Pharisees and the crowd refused to accept the evidence that was presented to them in the teaching and miracles of the Lord Jesus?

- What evidence is there today to the fact that Jesus is everything he claims he is?

For Prayer:

- Do you have a friend who is hardened to the evidence of Christ and his salvation? Take a moment to pray that

God would soften his or her heart to the facts presented to them in the Word of God.

- How did Jesus reveal himself to you? Thank him that he gave you eyes to see and ears to hear the evidence and accept what he said in his Word.

20

The Adulterous Woman

Read John 8:1–11

I t was dawn in the great city of Jerusalem. Jesus had come down from the Mount of Olives to the temple courtyard. People gathered around to hear him teach. They had heard much about his teaching. His fame had spread throughout the land. On this particular morning Jesus' teaching was interrupted when a group of Pharisees and teachers of the Law burst onto the scene. They were pushing a woman ahead of them as they approached. Those present shifted their attention from Jesus to what was happening before them. The group made its way to where Jesus was teaching. The woman was pushed in front of the crowd. Eyes focused on the woman. One man in the group spoke: "Teacher, this woman was caught in the act of adultery. In the Law, Moses commanded us to stone such women. Now what do you say?" (verses 4–5).

The fact of the matter was that they had not brought this woman to Jesus for his advice. They knew what the Law of

Moses stated; after all, these were the experts in the Law. They brought this woman to Jesus because they were looking for a means of accusing him. What would Jesus tell them? Would he suggest that they forgive her? If he did, they could accuse him of breaking the Law of Moses. Would Jesus suggest that they follow the letter of the Law and stone the woman? If he did, they could break the opinion the crowd had of him. The crowd saw in Jesus a friend of sinners. He had preached about life and love. They saw him as a man of compassion and healing. To see him pass the death sentence on this woman would have shattered their image of him.

One of the problems the Pharisees had with Jesus was that he had, according to them, broken the law of the Sabbath. If he chose to condemn this woman as the Law of Moses stated, they would, no doubt, have lost no time in accusing him of inconsistency. Why would he keep the Law of Moses regarding adultery and not the law of the Sabbath? The Pharisees and the teachers of the law were not altogether honest in the reason they were bringing this woman to him. They were using her to get to Jesus.

Jesus knew that the Jewish leaders were only trying to test him. In response he bent down and wrote on the ground. Why did Jesus write on the ground? This has perplexed commentators. There are several possible answers to this question.

One possible answer is that the Lord Jesus simply did not want to answer them. The King James Version of the Bible adds: *"as though he heard them not"* (verse 6). He understood their reason for bringing this woman to him. They were not seeking his advice; they were looking for a chance to kill him.

Another possible answer is that Jesus was writing something very particular on the ground. Maybe he was writing a passage of Scripture. Maybe he was writing down some of the sins of her accusers. Jesus saw their hypocrisy.

Maybe in his writing he was reminding them of their own guilt before God. Every eye would have been looking at what he was writing.

It may also be that the Lord was in prayer. Was he asking for wisdom from his Father? Was he waiting on him for words to say? We are not told.

The Jewish leaders pressed him for an answer. Finally, Jesus stood up and said: "If any one of you is without sin, let him be the first to throw a stone at her" (verse 7). Then Jesus stooped down and continued to write on the ground. He threw the ball back into their court. As he wrote in silence, it seemed that the Holy Spirit began his work. The moment was tense. The Pharisees and teachers of the law reasoned among themselves. What would they do? If they cast the stone, they were saying to all the people around them that they were without sin. They knew they could not say this. To say this would mean losing the respect of the people. One by one they began to leave until Jesus was left alone with the woman.

The only person present that day that could have cast the first stone was Jesus himself. He alone was without sin. What would be his judgment? Jesus stopped writing on the ground. "Woman, where are they? Has no one condemned you?" he asked (verse 10). "No one, sir," came the reply (verse 11). Jesus responded: "Then neither do I condemn you, . . . "Go now and leave your life of sin" (verse 11).

That day the life of that woman was saved. Had she been left to the Pharisees, they would have stoned her. Jesus is not like our fellow human beings. He is willing to forgive. The Pharisees had brought her to the only person who could have forgiven her sins. This guilty woman found forgiveness in the Lord Jesus. As she left Jesus that day, she knew her guilt. The Pharisees had publicly humiliated her. Her life in that community would never again be the same. She would be branded as an adulteress. When people looked at her from then on, they would see her in a very different light. There was the question of whether she could continue to live in the community. While it would have been very difficult for people to forgive and forget, the Lord Jesus, on the other hand, had already done so.

It is important to note here that while the Lord Jesus did forgive the woman of her sin, he told her that she was not to return to this sin again. The forgiveness came with an obligation. She was, from that point on, to guard her heart so that she did not fall into the same sin. This would not necessarily be easy. If we have been forgiven, we must not return to our sin. God expects us now to live in victory.

Today the arms of this same Jesus are open to receive us and to forgive us of our sins as well. It does not matter what we have done. There is no sin too large for the Lord to forgive.

For Consideration:

- What does this passage teach us about forgiveness?

- Is there someone who has wronged you? What challenge does this chapter bring to you?

- Are there sins that you have returned to? Maybe you have come many times to the Lord for forgiveness but still keep falling into this sin. What is this particular sin?

For Prayer:

- Ask God to help you to forgive those who have offended you.

- Thank God that he has forgiven you so completely that never again will those sins be held against you.

- Ask the Lord to give you complete victory over those sins that you seem to keep falling into.

21

Jesus, the Light of the World

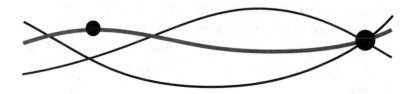

Read John 8:12–30

In John 8:12 the Lord Jesus made the claim to be the light of the world. "I am the light of the world. Whoever follows me will never walk in darkness, but have the light of life."

The Pharisees were present when Jesus made this statement. They challenged him on it. They claimed that what Jesus said was not valid because he spoke for himself. He had no witness to back up what he was saying. Unless he had a witness, no one could accept what he was saying as truth.

In response to this objection, Jesus reminded the Pharisees that even if he did speak on his own behalf, his testimony was still valid (verse 14). He knew the truth. He knew where he had come from. The Pharisees did not know him, nor did they know where he was from. It was their word against his, and they knew nothing about him.

In verse 15 Jesus reminded the Pharisees that they were

judging him by human standards. They were asking him for a human witness to his divinity. There was no one on earth who could qualify as a witness to this fact because no one on earth had seen Jesus with the Father before the creation of the world. No one had seen Jesus in his glory before he came to earth. No one had seen the Spirit of God place the Lord Jesus in the womb of Mary. No one was qualified to stand as a witness to Jesus in this regard.

Jesus reminded the Pharisees, however, that he was not without witness. God the Father stood as his witness (verse 16). The testimony of two people, according to the Law, was valid. Jesus was one witness and his Father was the other. The Father bore witness to the Son by his statement at his baptism by John. On that day, when the Holy Spirit of God fell on Jesus, those present heard a voice from heaven saying: "You are my Son, whom I love; with you I am well pleased" (Luke 3:22). What greater witness could there be than the witness of the creator of the universe who cannot lie?

Beyond this example, however, there was also the testimony of the works the Father did through the Son. Jesus clearly tells us that he did nothing of his own accord, but he only did what the Father told him to do (5:19). The works he did were a sign that the Father was in him (14:10–11).

This was not good enough for the Pharisees. "Where is your Father?" they asked (verse 19). "You do not know me or my Father," came the reply from Jesus. "If you knew me, you would know my Father also" (verse 19). Jesus went on to tell the disciples that he was going away to a place where they could not find him (verse 21). He was going to see his Father. The Pharisees would look for him, but they would never be able to find him because of their unbelief. They would die in their sins and be eternally separated from God. They were of this world. They had never been born again into the kingdom of God. They had rejected the Son of God as the light of the world. They could not see because they were still in the darkness of their sin and refused the light that God had put in their midst.

Notice how the scene has shifted. It was the Jews who had come to accuse Jesus. They were now the ones being accused. "I have much to say in judgment of you," said Jesus (verse 26). One day they would stand before the Father of all creation and account for their rejection of his Son.

The Pharisees understood nothing of what Jesus was telling them. Jesus told them that the time was coming when they would know that what he was telling them was true. "When you have lifted up the Son of Man, then you will know that I am the one I claim to be" Jesus told them (verse 28). This lifting up of the Son of Man referred to his crucifixion. The crucifixion of Christ would prove to the world that he was the Son of God. Through his death and resurrection, Jesus would prove to all that he was the conqueror of the grave. By his death, he would overcome Satan and the power of sin. Through his death, men and women all over the world would come to understand that they were sinners who could find forgiveness of those sins in his name.

The scene was like a court room. Jesus was the accused. The Pharisees were the accusers. The people were the jury. The accusers claimed that Jesus had no witness, and therefore his testimony was invalid. Jesus responded by reminding them that they had not produced any evidence to prove him wrong. As for their claim that he had no witness, they were incorrect. Jesus called upon his Father, the creator and sustainer of all life, who cannot lie. His Father stood beside him as a witness to the validity of the testimony of his Son. Jesus reminded them also that his death would prove that he was who he claimed to be.

As time has passed, this statement of Jesus has proven to be true. Countless men and women the world over have been impacted by the death of the Lord Jesus. Multitudes have attested to the fact that it was this death that set them free from the power of darkness. Lives have been radically changed through the power of his cross.

Even as he spoke, the people were coming to their verdict. Verse 30 tells us that men and women were putting their trust in him. They cast their vote in favor of the Lord Jesus, surrendering to the light.

The Pharisees had hoped that they could cast doubt on the Lord Jesus. Their accusations only served to draw men and women to him. They, the accusers, now stood accused before him. The day is coming when we will all have to answer to God for what we have done with his Son.

For Consideration:

- Why is it so hard for some people to accept the Lord Jesus today?

- What evidence is there that the Lord Jesus is everything he claims to be?

- How do you know personally that the Lord Jesus is who he says he is?

- What evidence is there of the light of Christ in your life?

- What is the difference between living in the darkness of sin and living in the light of Christ?

For Prayer:

- Ask the Lord to reveal any areas of darkness in your life. Confess these sins and yield to his light.

- Thank the Lord that he has revealed himself to you as the light of the world.

- Thank him that because of his work on the cross, you can stand confidently before the Father, forgiven of all your sin.

22

The True Disciple

Read John 8:31–32

What is a disciple? What are the signs of true discipleship? In these two short verses Jesus gives us three characteristics of the true disciple. First, Jesus tells us that the true disciple is one who holds to his teaching: "If you hold to my teaching, you are really my disciples" (verse 31). If your heart has no desire to hold to and obey the Word of God, then you cannot be assured that you are a child of God. Notice here the word "continue" (KJV) or "hold to" (NIV). These words imply perseverance. They imply that the person doing the "holding" will encounter difficulty. They remind us that not everything will be easy in the Christian life. The true believer, however, is obedient, even if it means struggle or death. John reminds us of this important truth in each of the letters to the seven churches in the book of Revelation. Consider these passages, for example:

> To him who overcomes, I will give the right to
> eat from the tree of life. (Revelation 2:7)

> He who overcomes will not be hurt by the
> second death. (Revelation 2:11)

> Him who overcomes I will make a pillar in
> the temple of my God. (Revelation 3:12)

The true believer, according to these verses, is one who perseveres or holds on till the end.

There is something about accepting Jesus as our Lord and Savior that changes our lives. The Holy Spirit has a radical impact on the lives of believers. He renews hearts. He gives a new desire to obey the Lord and live for him. Sometimes this will bring suffering, but believers patiently endure, though at times they may falter. True disciples of Jesus Christ desire to follow their master, whatever the cost. True disciples willingly deny themselves for Christ. The greatest desire of true believers is to be faithful to the Lord Jesus.

One clear test of true discipleship is that a person's heart has been renewed and there is a real desire to serve and follow the Lord Jesus. The true disciple will continue to hold to the Word of Christ, no matter the cost. A disciple will suffer, if need be, rather than be unfaithful to that Word. You can recognize a true disciple by obedience to the Word of the Lord.

A second test is that the true disciple is one who knows the truth (verse 31). Jesus told the Jewish leaders that they did not accept his Word because they did not know the Father. Only those who had chosen to do the will of the Father would know that what he taught was of God: "If anyone chooses to do God's will, he will find out whether my teaching comes from God or whether I speak on my own" (7:17).

The true disciple has a natural assurance of the truth of the Word of God. This comes from the fact that the Holy Spirit lives in the believer. The Spirit confirms the Word of God to us. The apostle Paul, on the road to Damascus, was confronted by the living Christ. After his confrontation with Christ, Paul's belief system was radically changed. What he formerly fought against now became a passion in his life. All doubt   ed concerning Jesus and his teaching. The Spirit of God, who had come to live in Paul's heart, confirmed to him the truth of Jesus' teachings. The same thing happens to all who come to the Lord Jesus. One of the ministries of the Spirit of God is to convince us of the teachings of the Lord Jesus. Anyone who has this Spirit will recognize the truth of the Word of God.

John 10:27 reminds us that true sheep recognize the voice of the Good Shepherd. They will run away from the voice of another shepherd. To be a true disciple is to be able to recognize the voice of the Master. It is to be able to distinguish his voice from all others. This does not mean that as believers we will never have differences of opinion regarding the interpretation of the Word of God. There is, however, in each of us a deep conviction of the truth of the words of Scripture and belief in the person and work of Christ. There is a level of intimacy that exists between Jesus and his sheep. There is communion and fellowship between them. The true disciple knows the words that Jesus spoke are true and worthy of full confidence. This assurance is the result of the work of the Holy Spirit in their lives.

Finally, the true believer has been set free by the truth: "Then you will know the truth, and the truth will set you free" (verse 32). The truth has a profound impact on the life of the believer. This truth has set the believer free. There are a number of ways in which this freedom is evident.

First, believers have been set free from the wrath of God by the truth. There was a time in the lives of believers when they were separated from God. One day they came face to face with the truth that the Lord Jesus died on the cross for their sins. They learned how they could be forgiven. They learned how the Lord Jesus died so that they could enter into the presence of a Holy God. The reality of this truth changed their lives. This truth pointed them to the solution to the problem of separation from God. When believers accepted this truth and stepped out in faith, they were forgiven and brought into a right relationship with the Father.

Second, believers have been set free from an endless search for meaning and purpose. They found their true identity in the truth of Christ. On the pages of Scripture, they were introduced to the only One who could fill the emptiness of their souls. Here in this truth they finally came to an end of their search for meaning and purpose in life. Jesus was the answer to the emptiness of their souls.

Third, true disciples have been set free from the power of sin in their lives. On the pages of Scripture, they have discovered how they can overcome sin. They have learned that the Holy Spirit of God lives in them. They have understood that they no longer have to be defeated by Satan. When attacked by the lies of Satan, they can draw the sword of the Word from its sheath and confront these lies head on. They have learned from this truth what is right and acceptable to God the Father. This Word has become comfort in the midst of discouragement and a guide in the midst of temptation. By living according to this Word, they have lived in victory over the enemy. They have been freed from the power of sin.

The true disciple, according to Jesus, has three characteristics: continuing (persevering) in the words of Christ, recognizing and accepting the truth of the Word of God, and being set free by this truth from the power of sin and evil. Are you a true disciple?

For Consideration:

- In what way has Satan been seeking to stand against the truth of the Word of God in your life and in your society?

- Our enemy has spent much time and effort on opposing the Word of God. What does this tell us about the importance of the Word of God in defeating the enemy?

- How has the Word of God set you free?

- Take a moment to review the three characteristics of the true believer as outlined here in this section. Do you see evidence of these characteristics in your own life?

For Prayer:

- Do you recall when you came to the knowledge of the truth of the Word of God? Thank the Lord that he gave you an understanding of truth.

- Ask the Lord to reveal to you any areas of your life where you have believed the lies of the enemy. Ask him to give you grace to surrender to what you know to be true in the Scriptures.

23

A Child or a Slave?

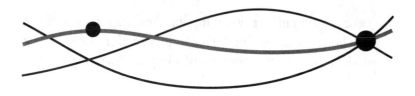

Read John 8:33–59

J esus had reminded the Jewish leaders that the truth he taught them would set them free (verses 31–32). The Jews did not understand why they needed to be set free. They were descendants of Abraham. They did not see themselves as slaves to anyone. There are many people in our day like these Jews. They cling to their upbringing or their church affiliation. They do not see that they are sinners in need of a Savior. They sincerely believe that being born into a Christian family or going to a Christian church is all that it takes to get to heaven.

To help the Jewish leaders to understand why they needed to be set free, Jesus reminded them that whoever committed sin was a servant of sin (verse 34). There is not one of us who has not committed sin. We have all been stained by sin and its effects in our lives. Sin has held each and every one of us in its grip. We have all been slaves to sin.

Jesus explained to the Jewish leaders the difference

between a slave and a child. Unlike a son or a daughter, the slave did not have a place in the family. The slave may have been associated with the family and may even have been very involved in the life of that family, but a slave was not part of it. A slave would not inherit the blessings of the family members.

Before we came to Jesus to be forgiven of our sin, we were not part of the family of God. We may have been around Christians and have been in many Christian activities, but we were still a slave of sin and not a family member. There are many who believe that they will inherit the eternal blessings of the Father, but they have never become his child. There are many who serve the family of God who, in reality, have no part in it.

John 1:12 reminds us that only those who have received the Lord Jesus Christ and believe on his name will be given the right to become children of God. Only Jesus can set us free from the slavery of sin. The Jews who listened to Jesus that day claimed to be children of Abraham and therefore children of God. They could not understand why Jesus would tell them that they needed to be set free. They served the Lord as slaves and servants, but they would not inherit the blessings of the Father. They were servants, but they were not children.

Jesus knew that the Jews were ready to kill him because they rejected his teaching (verse 37). To Jesus these two facts alone proved that they were not his disciples and therefore not part of the family of God. If they were true disciples and children of God, they would have known that what he was saying was true. (See verses 31–32.) "'If you were Abraham's children,' said Jesus, 'then you would do the things Abraham did'" (verse 39). If they were truly part of the family of God, they would not be fighting against Jesus and seeking to kill him. They were not the true children of

God. The Jews could not understand what Jesus was telling them.

The Jews present that day told Jesus that the only Father they had was God himself (verse 41). "If God were your Father, you would love me, for . . . . I have not come on my own; but he sent me," Jesus replied (verse 42). Jesus went on to explain to them that the reason why they could not understand what he meant was because they had never been born into the family of God. He told them that they were like their true father, the devil (verse 44).

Like their father, the devil, they chose to reject the truth in favor of a lie. Satan is the father of lies. He hates the truth. The Jews of Jesus' day turned their backs on him. God himself spoke to them, but they rejected his word. Like their father, the devil, who was a murderer from the beginning, they too wanted to kill the Son of God. Their father's lying and murderous blood owed through their veins. All evidence proved that Jesus was exactly who he said he was. The Jews, however, could not believe the truth. If they belonged to God they would have believed the truth, but instead they believed the lies their father, the devil, spoke to them.

Jesus' teaching caused quite a stir among the Jews present that day. They responded to him by calling him a Samaritan (verse 48). The Jews hated the Samaritans. They were calling him a Samaritan in order to insult him. To the Jew, the Samaritan was the lowest form of human life. This was how they perceived our Lord. Calling our Lord a Samaritan, however, was not enough. They told him that he was also demon-possessed. To these individuals, Jesus was worse than a Samaritan. He was a Samaritan possessed by a demon of hell.

"I am not possessed by a demon," responded Jesus (verse 49). He reminded the Jewish leaders that the judgment was coming. Only those who kept his commandments would be freed from that death (verse 51). By death he meant an eternal separation from God. He was telling these people that the day was coming when they would be judged for their refusal to accept the Lord Jesus. Despite these words, the Jews persisted in unbelief. To these leaders, Jesus was telling them that he was greater than their father Abraham. This was something they could not handle. "Who do you think you are?" they asked him insultingly (verse 53).

Jesus reminded the Jews that he was not seeking to glorify himself (verse 54). His heavenly Father would lift him up at the appropriate time. He told them that Abraham their father longed to see this very day (verse 56). God had communicated to Abraham that one day the Messiah would come. Abraham was even asked to offer his own son as a sacrifice on the altar, just as God would offer his Son. (See Genesis 22.)

Jesus spoke as though he knew Abraham. "You are not yet fifty years old," the Jews said to him, "and you have seen Abraham!" For the Jews, none of the things Jesus was saying made sense. "Before Abraham was born, I am," responded Jesus (verse 58). God had used this expression in Exodus 3: 14 when he called himself "I am." Jesus identified himself as God by using this expression. That was the last straw for the Jews. They picked up stones to kill Jesus. However, Jesus escaped from them.

By rejecting Jesus, they rejected his Father. By rejecting God, they proved that they were not his children. They were still slaves to sin. They believed the lie of Satan that because they were Abraham's children, they were automatically God's children. Satan continues to spread this lie today. He tells individuals that because they grew up in a Christian family, they are also part of God's family. He tells them that because they belong to a church, they also belong to God. He tells them that because they were baptized, they are God's children.

Slaves serve the family but do not belong to it. They

will not inherit the wealth of the family because they are not connected to that family by blood. Though once a slave, we became blood relations. Only the blood of Christ could cleanse us and change our status.

For Consideration:

- When did you become a son or daughter of Christ? What evidence of this is in your life?

- Are there lies of the enemy that you have been hearing and believing? What are they?

- What evidence is there that people still believe the lies of Satan in our day? What are the lies our society believes?

For Prayer:

- Ask God to open your mind to the lies of the enemy when they come your way.

- Take a moment to thank the Lord that he adopted you as a slave and made you his child.

- Thank the Lord for the blessings of being a child of God. Name your blessings and thank the Lord for them.

24

Go Wash

Read John 9:1–7

On one occasion Jesus and his disciples saw a man blind from birth. As they passed by the man, the disciples asked Jesus a question: "Rabbi, who sinned, this man or his parents, that he was born blind?" (verse 2). This statement reveals something about the belief of the disciples. They believed that God was punishing either this man or his family for some secret, personal sin.

There are times when sickness is the result of personal sin in our lives. In 1 Corinthians 11, Paul challenged the church in Corinth about their attitudes in the practice of the Lord's Supper. Some were partaking in an unworthy manner. As a result many members of the church were weak and sickly. The indication here is that they were sick and even dying because they were not respecting the Lord and his table. In the example before us in John 9, however, Jesus told his disciples that this was not the case with this man.

Neither this man nor his parents were guilty of sin. He was blind so that God's power could be shown in his life.

The God who permitted this blindness had a reason for it. Nothing in life is without a purpose. You may not understand why God has allowed something to happen to you. Be assured that, while you may not see it now, there is a reason for whatever God allows. He will work out whatever you suffer for your good and his glory.

In this case, God wanted to show his glory in the life of this man through physical healing. Like Jeremiah the prophet and John the Baptist, the blind man had been chosen before birth for a particular task. For forty years the prophet Jeremiah labored under tremendous obstacles. He saw one man after another reject him and his message. The blind man before us had never seen. His role, however, was no less important. His healing would impact many people. Through him, men and women would come to see the power of God. Sometimes the tasks to which the Lord calls us are very difficult. For some it will mean rejection. For others it will mean physical suffering. God took this man's eyesight. What would you be willing to give so that the glory of God would be revealed in you?

Jesus reminded his disciples that he had to do the work of him who sent him while it was still day because the night was coming when no one could work (verse 4). He told them that he was the light of the world. Jesus was telling the disciples that time was running short. He needed to do the works of his Father while it was still day. The time was coming when that light would be removed. Jesus, the light of the world, would leave them. While he was here, there was still much work to be done. The healing of this blind man was one of the works his Father had given him to do.

It is important that we understand that Jesus only did what the Father told him to do. He knew that it was the will of the Father to heal this man. We understand this by the way Jesus told the disciples that this man's sickness was not the result of sin but so that the glory of the Father could be revealed.

What is important here for us to note is that the Lord Jesus did not take matters into his own hands. He only did what the Father led him to do. How important it is for us to follow the example of the Lord Jesus here. Those of us who are in ministry know how easy it is for us to do things in our own way. How much further ahead would we be today if we would only start each day by seeking the will of the Father before moving ahead?

Having told the disciples that it was the will of the Father that this man be healed, the Lord "spit on the ground, made some mud with the saliva, and put it on the man's eyes" (verse 6). We are not told why Jesus did this. When the nobleman came to Jesus to ask him to heal his son, Jesus did not even go with him to see his son. (See John 4.) Jesus healed his son at a distance. It was not necessary for the Lord to physically touch an individual for him to be healed.

This encounter teaches us that the Lord does not always work with us all in the same way. Jesus healed the nobleman's son at a distance. He healed this man by applying mud to his eyes. He raised Lazarus from the dead by calling out to him. He healed the lame and the sick by physically touching them. By simply touching the hem of Jesus' garment, one lady was healed. Jesus deals with each of us on an individual basis. You are not another article on the assembly line. He knows you by name, and he deals with you individually and personally.

Though Jesus put mud on the eyes of this blind man, the man was not immediately healed. This was not because Jesus had failed. Not all healing is instant. Everything was in place for the healing. God had chosen the man for healing. The Lord Jesus had touched him. The healing mud was on his eyes, but he was not yet healed. What was the problem?

The problem was that Jesus had told him to go to the pool of Siloam to wash. While everything was in place, nothing would happen until the man stepped out in faith and washed in the pool of Siloam.

The act of washing in the pool was an act of faith. In the days of Elisha the prophet, a man by the name of Naaman came to him to be healed of his leprosy (2 Kings 5). Elisha told him to go and wash in the River Jordan seven times and he would be healed. Naaman was insulted. He was returning home when his servant convinced him that he should do exactly what the prophet said. Naaman swallowed his pride and went to the river to wash. When he came out of the water the seventh time, Naaman was healed just as Elisha had said. Before his healing could take place, Naaman had to surrender to the God of Israel and do what he said. He could have walked away from his healing. It would have been easy for the blind man to say, "What's the use. If I'm not healed now I won't be healed just because I wash my face." He could have walked away and refused the healing that the Lord wanted to give him.

How many people are just one step away from their healing today? I have heard people say: "If God wanted to give me victory, he could do so without me having to go to someone else?" "If God wanted to save me, he could do it without me ever stepping foot inside that church." "If God wanted to draw me closer to himself, he could do so without me ever having to go to that conference." All these things are true, but is that how the Lord wants to do it for you? Could it be that the means by which God wants to heal you or renew you is by having you humble yourself and go to someone else? Jesus could have healed that blind man that day without him having to go to the pool of Siloam—but he didn't. How does he want to deal with you? Don't hinder what God wants to do in your life by being stubborn and refusing to do what God is telling you to do. If God wants you to go to the pool, then go to the pool. If God wants you to humble yourself, then humble yourself. Don't harden your heart.

We don't have to continue in our blindness when everything has been done for our healing? Like the blind man, take that step of faith and experience everything that God has for you to experience.

For Consideration:

- Why do you suppose that God wants us sometimes to take a step of faith before releasing his blessing?

- Take a moment to consider the major things God has done in your life? Was there any way in which you too had to step out in faith before experiencing that victory?

- Does God work in every person in the same way? What does this section of Scripture teach us about God's way of dealing with each of us?

- Have there been times in your life when you have not taken that step of faith? What was the result?

For Prayer:

- Ask God to forgive you for the times when you walked away from what he was asking you to do, and you did not experience his blessing in your life.

- Ask him to make you willing to do things his way and not your way.

- Thank the Lord for the way he treats us all individually. Thank him that he knows each of us personally and will deal with us in a very personal way.

25

Spiritual Sight

Read John 9:8–38

Jesus had healed a man born blind. Though he had been physically healed, there was still the question of his spiritual sight. Jesus had not yet finished with this man.

When his neighbors saw that this man had been healed, they were divided among themselves. "Isn't this the same man who used to sit and beg?" they asked (verse 8). Some believed it was him. Others felt it was someone else. They had never expected this man to see again. Their problem was not that they did not recognize him; it was their unbelief in the miracle.

The crowd asked the healed man to explain what had happened to him. He assured them that he was the blind beggar they all knew. "How then were your eyes opened?" they asked (verse 10). He told them how the Lord Jesus had anointed his eyes with mud and told him to go and wash in the pool of Siloam. When he obeyed, he was healed of his blindness.

"Where is this man?" they asked (verse 12). "I don't know," was his reply. This conversation between the people and the beggar was important. The man born blind knew very little about Jesus. To him Jesus was simply the man who had healed him. He did not know his name or where he lived.

The people brought the healed man to the Jewish leaders to see what they had to say. They too asked him how he was healed. "He put mud on my eyes, . . . and I washed, and now I see," he told them (verse 15). Because this miracle had happened on the Sabbath, the Jewish leaders were divided. Some said that because he healed on the Sabbath, it was not possible that Jesus could be from God. They could not believe that someone from God would break their interpretation of the Sabbath. Others claimed that no sinner could possibly do what Jesus did if he were not from God. They turned to the man born blind and asked his opinion. This put him in a very delicate position. He was bound to offend someone.

Everyone awaited his response. "He is a prophet," the man said (verse 17). His answer showed that he had not yet come to fully understand who Jesus was. He did believe, however, that the power of God was evident in Jesus. For this reason he called Jesus a prophet.

The leaders began to question whether the man before them ever was blind (verse 18). They were not sure what they thought about this miracle and were looking for a means to explain it away. The leaders sent for the healed man's parents. When they arrived, the leaders asked them if this was their son who had been born blind. The parents reassured the Jewish leaders that he was indeed their son and that he had been born blind. When asked how he had been healed, however, the parents declined to answer. They did not want to get involved in a discussion over the person of Jesus. The Pharisees had already made it plain to everyone that whoever acknowledged Jesus as the Christ would be put out of the synagogue (verse 22). His parents did not want this to happen.

Again, the leaders called the man for further questioning. This time their approach was more direct. "'Give glory to God,' they said. 'We know this man is a sinner,'" (verse 24). The healed man replied: "Whether he is a sinner or not, I do not know. One thing I do know. I was blind but now I see!" His mind was not clear about the identity of Jesus, but he did know that Jesus had done something in his life. Many times we will not have all the answers. Who among us can, in reality, explain the work of God? Can you explain how or why God does what he does? While we may not be able to explain to others why God does what he does, we can certainly tell them what he has done and how he has changed our lives. This is what the healed man was doing.

Unhappy with the answer, the Jews continued their interrogation. They asked him again how he was healed (verse 26). The patience of the healed man was wearing thin. "I have told you already, and you did not listen. Why do you want to hear it again? Do you want to become his disciples, too?" That statement cut the Jews very deeply. They took serious offence at this and responded in anger. They "hurled insults at him" (verse 28). Then they said: "You are this fellow's disciple! We are disciples of Moses! We know that God spoke to Moses, but as for this fellow, we don't even know where he comes from." With these words, the Jewish leaders separated themselves completely from what Jesus had accomplished in restoring the sight of the blind beggar. The Jews showed great zeal for what they believed to be truth but no compassion for the man who had been healed. They could not rejoice in his new-found sight because they were too busy defending their concept of truth. Somehow we must find a balance between truth and compassion in our lives.

The healed man confronted the Pharisees: "You don't know where he comes from, yet he opened my eyes" (verse 30). He went on to tell the Pharisees that God does not listen to the sinner but to the godly person who does his will. This tells us that the healed man saw Jesus not only as a prophet but also as a godly person who was doing the will of the Father. The Father answered the prayers of Jesus because he was living in his will. To the man born blind, the only way to explain the miracle he had just experienced was that Jesus was from God, doing the will of the heavenly Father. "If this man were not from God, he could do nothing," he told them (verse 33).

When they heard this, the Pharisees responded: "You were steeped in sin at birth; how dare you lecture us!" (verse 34). The Pharisees believed what the disciples had believed. (See verse 2.) They believed that this man's blindness was the result of some personal sin in his life. They felt that God was punishing him for that sin. How could a lowly sinner as he was even pretend to teach them? There was nothing he could teach them. Their minds were closed. They were so angry with him that they threw him out of the synagogue. He would be an outcast from that day forth.

When Jesus heard that the healed man had been thrown out of the synagogue, he made a special effort to see him. "Do you believe in the Son of Man?" asked Jesus (verse 35). "Who is he, sir," responded the man. He really did not know. "He is the one speaking to you," answered Jesus (verse 37). Those words struck home. "Lord, I believe," said the man, and he fell down and worshiped Jesus. Something happened that moment. Unseen to the human eye, the hand of God was touching the spiritual eyes of this man and giving him spiritual sight.

Now he understood who Jesus was. He had defended him before the Pharisees but had not known who he really was. He had been put out of the synagogue and had suffered for the name of the Lord Jesus without knowing him as Lord and

Savior. On meeting Jesus that day, God's full purpose was accomplished in his life—physical and spiritual healing.

Are there those around you that may be serving Jesus without really knowing him? Maybe they have stood up for him at work or at school. Maybe they have suffered for their stand on religious or spiritual matters. They are like the healed man, serving a person they do not really know. What a difference it made in the life of this man to understand who Jesus really was. He would continue to serve him and defend his name, but now his service would take on a new meaning.

This blind beggar gained sight that day which the religious leaders of his day lacked. For all their education and experience, they did not have what this man had. He saw Jesus as the Son of God, while the Pharisees rejected him. This man would live for eternity in the presence of the Jesus who had healed him. The Pharisees would perish and spend an eternity separated from God. The Pharisees, with all their religious traditions and doctrines, did not see what this man saw that day.

For Consideration:

- What did it take for the blind man to come to know the Lord? Was his physical healing sufficient to bring him to an understanding of who Jesus really was? What was the relationship between his physical healing and his ultimate salvation?

- What was the difference between the blind man's relationship with Jesus prior to meeting him in the temple and after meeting him?

- Can you recall the day you met the Lord Jesus and accepted him as your Lord and Savior? What difference did that make in your life? How did you see things differently?

For Prayer:

- Do you know someone who, like the healed man, defends the cause of Jesus without really knowing him? Ask the Lord to reveal himself to this individual in a special way.

- Thank the Lord that he healed your spiritual blindness and showed himself to you as Lord and Savior.

26

Self-Inflicted Blindness

Read John 9:39–41

J esus' discussion with the man born blind was coming to an end. The Pharisees had been present during this interaction. They struggled with what Jesus was saying. He was claiming to be the Son of Man (verse 35). To the Pharisee this was blasphemy.

Here in this next section Jesus told those present why he had come to earth: "For judgment I have come into this world, so that the blind will see and those who see will become blind." We need to take a moment to examine what Jesus meant by this statement.

We have no problem understanding the fact that Jesus came to give spiritual eyesight to those who were lost in their sins. Jesus had given this spiritual eyesight to the man born blind. This man had been living in spiritual darkness. He had not known the Lord Jesus and the means of salvation. When Jesus opened his spiritual eyes, the man understood for the first time that Jesus was the Christ, the Son of God who had come to save him from his sin. The light shone in. The healed man was enlightened to his need of Jesus and the salvation he offered. The man opened up his heart and surrendered to the work of God's Holy Spirit. That day his life was changed.

What did Jesus mean when he told his listeners that he had also come so that "those who see will become blind" (verse 39)? In the story of the healing of the blind beggar, the Pharisees had boasted that they were the ones who had spiritual insight. They were the teachers of the law. They were the enlightened ones. They looked down on the man born blind, claiming that he did not know anything (verse 34). They did not believe that this beggar had anything to teach them. Neither did they believe that Jesus had anything to teach them. These were the individuals who would be made blind.

In the story before us, we see an example of what Jesus was communicating. The blind man was made to see the reality of Jesus in his life. Those who claimed to see were revealed for what they really were—spiritually blind. Even this simple beggar could see past the supposed wisdom of the Pharisees. Jesus exposed their spiritual blindness to the world.

The Pharisees, as blind as they were, immediately picked up on what Jesus was saying. "What? Are we blind too?" they asked (verse 40). Jesus responded: "If you were blind, you would not be guilty of sin; but now that you claim you can see, your guilt remains" (verse 41). We need to examine this verse in greater detail.

Jesus told the Pharisees that if they were blind, they would not be guilty of sin. Does this mean that if they had never heard the message of the gospel, they would not be held accountable for their sin? This can hardly be the case. If this were the case, Jesus would never have needed to die for our sins. If by remaining in its blindness the world could be innocent before God, it would be best for us to abandon the call of God and leave the world in darkness. This is not the call of God, however. Jesus came to reveal the truth. He came to preach the good news of salvation.

To understand what Jesus is telling us here, we must interpret this verse in light of the rest of Scripture. In Romans 1:18–21 we read: "The wrath of God is being revealed from heaven against the godlessness and wickedness of men who suppress the truth by their wickedness, since what may be known about God is plain to them, because God has made it plain to them. For since the creation of the world God's invisible qualities—his eternal power and divine nature—have been clearly seen, being understood from what has been made, so that men are without excuse" (Romans 1:18–21).

Paul tells us here that God has revealed himself to all people. Though men and women may never have heard the name of Jesus, the character of God is obvious in creation. Through creation we understand the power and nature of God. The only way for us to be blind to God is if we willfully turn our backs on the powerful evidence around us. God gives us every breath we breathe. Every beat of our hearts is a reminder that God exists. All of creation shouts that God is alive. God has created us in his own image. Each of us has a soul that is able to commune with God. By our very nature, we crave spiritual meaning. Our whole being cries out for God. Spiritual blindness is the result of turning our backs on the knowledge that God gives us. No one will be condemned without reason. We are condemned because, like the Pharisees, we reject the evidence that is all around us.

The Pharisees and the Jews of Jesus' day rejected the evidence that God had given them. They claimed to know the truth but turned their backs on the Lord Jesus. They felt they had a better way. If God had not created them in his image with a hunger for spiritual reality and revealed himself to them by means of his Word and his creation, he could not have legitimately condemned them. Humans are different from animals in that they have been created with a spiritual nature. An animal is not created in the image of God. An animal does not have a soul. Animals live in darkness with no hope of eternal life or relationship with their creator. Animals die and cease to exist. There is no place of eternal punishment for animals. They live on this earth and die and are no more. God does not judge them. This is not true for people. We are spiritual creatures created for God and will one day have to account for our actions (Ephesians 1:5–6; Hebrews 4:13).

God has spoken very loudly to mankind of his existence. The Pharisees saw the evidence around them. The Lord Jesus had healed the blind man before them. They heard the Lord Jesus speak to them about coming from God. Beyond this, they also had the testimony of the Scriptures they studied. Despite all this evidence, the Pharisees completely turned their backs on the Lord Jesus. They saw the Messiah but rejected him. If God had never spoken to them through creation, their inner nature, the Scriptures and a whole host of other means, maybe they could legitimately claim to be blind and excused. However, they were without excuse because God had clearly shown himself to them.

The reality of the matter is that all of us are without excuse for rejecting Jesus. There is ample evidence to prove that Jesus is as he claimed to be. No one can ever claim innocence before him. It is impossible not to see evidence of God. We are not condemned because God has never revealed himself to us. We are condemned because, after seeing the evidence, we reject it.

Jesus came so that those who could not see would be healed and given new sight. He came also so that those who claimed to see and were misleading others would be exposed for their evil.

For Consideration:

- What evidence is there of the reality of a personal God around us today?

- Can anyone ever truly claim to be spiritually blind to the presence of a personal God in this world?

- How did God reveal himself to you personally?

For Prayer:

- Thank the Lord for the way he has revealed himself to you in his Word and in creation.

- Do you have friends who have been resisting the Lord? Take a moment to ask the Lord to open their eyes to the reality of a personal God.

27

The Good Shepherd

Read John 10:1–21

In John 10 the Lord Jesus compared himself to a Shepherd. Through this illustration, the Lord Jesus taught some very important spiritual truths about himself and our relationship with him.

Jesus began by stating that anyone who does not enter the sheep pen by the door is a thief and a robber (verse 1). The sheep pen is a place of security and shelter for the sheep. Jesus seems to be using the pen to illustrate many different aspects of salvation. In verse 1 we see that the sheep are to enter this pen through a certain gate. Verse 7 tells us that Jesus is the door to this sheepfold of salvation. If you want to experience the security and shelter of salvation, you will need to go through the Lord Jesus. There are many ways people try to get into this sheep pen. Some try church attendance. Others try good works. They believe that if they go to church enough or do enough good deeds, then God will accept them. Jesus is telling us that anyone who tries to be saved from judgment by any of these means is the same as a thief or robber. They are not welcome into the fold. They are impostors. They are not true believers. The true believer will come through the door. The true believer is one who understands that the only way into the salvation of God is through the work of the Lord Jesus Christ.

In Bible times shepherds would bring their sheep to a pen at night. The shepherds would hire someone to stand watch at the door all night. When the shepherds arrived early in the morning to take their sheep to pasture, the sheep of all the shepherds would be mingled together. In order to separate the sheep, shepherds would simply use their voices. Sheep would recognize the voice of their own shepherd. When they heard their own shepherd's voice, these sheep would make their way to the sound of that voice and be led out to pasture. Sheep will not listen to the voice of a stranger. They will run away from any other shepherd who tries to call them. They respond only to the voice of their own shepherd.

This is a real challenge for us as believers who have experienced the wonderful salvation of God. There are many voices all around us. These voices call us to experience life at its fullest. They tempt us to turn, if just for a moment, away from the principles of the Word of God. Those who truly belong to the Good Shepherd will run away from these voices. They follow only one voice—the voice of the Lord Jesus.

Notice here that there is a close relationship between the shepherd and the sheep. The shepherd is able to recognize each sheep. A good shepherd knows each sheep in the ock by name.

While Jesus is interested in his church as a whole, he is particularly interested in us as individuals. He knows our names. He knows the number of hairs on our heads (Matthew 10:30). He knows when things are not going right for us. He knows when we are suffering and he cares deeply.

We have seen how Jesus compared himself to the gate (verse 7). Jesus warned his audience, however, that there were many people who claimed to have another way of salvation. Jesus was clear here: "All who ever came before me were thieves and robbers" (verse 8). These individuals did not belong in the fold. They were seeking to mislead the sheep. Even in the days when the Lord Jesus walked on this earth, those "thieves and robbers" were evident. Jesus often came into con ict with the Pharisees, who set themselves up as shepherds of God's people. In reality they were misleading God's people by turning them from the True Shepherd. Even in our day there may be false shepherds in our midst. Jesus alone is the True Shepherd. He alone can care for us and provide for us the full salvation of God. Jesus reminds us that his sheep will not be easily deceived. They will recognize these false shepherds. The Spirit of God will reveal this to them as they examine the truth of the Scripture.

In verse 9 we see yet another aspect to the salvation that the Lord offers. Notice here that the shepherd leads his sheep out into rich pastures. Not only does Jesus lead us into the sheepfold of salvation, he also leads us from that place into the pastures of abundant life. (See verse 10.) The Lord has much more in store for us than just that one-time experience of salvation. Salvation is just the beginning. Imagine the sheep being content to stay all day in the sheepfold. What joys they would be missing. The pastures of abundant life are teaming with fresh grass and refreshing waters. The Good Shepherd wants to lead his people from that place of salvation into the joy of service and fellowship with him. There is more to a marriage than just the wedding. Salvation, like the wedding, brings us into a wonderful relationship. Now that we have experienced that relationship with the Lord Jesus, we must move from there to new heights of fellowship and service.

Admittedly, it takes a certain amount of courage to step out from the fold, but the Lord has promised to lead us. If we are willing to follow the Shepherd into this unknown territory, he will eventually lead us to refreshing pastures and quiet streams.

Notice in this section that there are things that characterize the relationship between the sheep and the shepherd. First, the sheep can distinguish the voice of their shepherd from all other voices (verse 3). The Spirit of God, dwelling within the hearts of believers, enables them to know the voice of Christ in the midst of a whole host of worldly voices seeking to be heard.

Second, the shepherd goes ahead of his sheep and leads them (verse 3). While there may be many struggles and difficulties for us as believers, we can be assured that the shepherd who goes ahead of us will protect us from danger. We can step out with confidence because the Good Shepherd has gone before us to fend off the enemy.

Third, the sheep will not listen to the voice of another (verse 5). While there are many temptations along the way, the sheep have a one-track mind. They will only listen to the familiar sound of their shepherd's voice. They run away from the voice of another shepherd. This ought to characterize our relationship with the Good Shepherd today. We should be able to recognize his voice and follow him alone. We should be able to turn our backs on the other voices crying out for attention. We too need to have a "one-track" mind.

So deep and intense is the devotion of the Shepherd to his sheep that he would willingly give up his life for his sheep (verse 11). A false shepherd would not willingly lay down his life for the sheep. If a wolf came into the fold, the hired hand or the false shepherd would run for cover. The Good Shepherd, however, would willingly lay down his life to save even one of these sheep.

Is it not amazing that a shepherd would have such

devotion for his sheep? It is hard to imagine that a human being would die to save the life of a single animal. How much more beyond our understanding is that the Lord Jesus, the Son of God, would lay down his life for you and me? Why would a holy God die for sinful people? This is a mystery we may never fully understand.

As the Good Shepherd, Jesus knows all of his sheep (verse 14). There were other sheep that were not yet in the fold of Judaism. These sheep were from various nations and tribes. We Gentiles are some of those sheep that Jesus spoke of that day. Jesus knew them all. He would also call out to them, and they too would hear his voice and follow him.

Jesus willingly laid down his life for his sheep on the cross. No one took his life. The religious leaders of the day thought that they had, in themselves, authority to take the life of the Lord Jesus. This was not the case. Jesus offered his life freely for you and me (verse 18). He did this in obedience to the command and purpose of his Father.

When the Jews heard what Jesus was telling them, they were divided in their opinion of him. Some claimed he had a demon and that he had gone mad. They tried to discourage others from listening to him (verse 20). There were others in the crowd that day who were not so sure that he was demon-possessed. They wondered how a demon could have actually made the blind man to see. While they did not necessarily accept him as the Son of God, they were at least opening their eyes and ears to the facts that were being presented to them.

For Consideration:

• What does this passage teach us about Jesus being the only way of salvation? In what ways do people in our day try to merit salvation?

- Is salvation an end in itself? What does God expect from us now that we have come to him?

- How can we distinguish the voice of the Lord from the voices that cry out for our attention each day?

- If the Good Shepherd is willing to give his life for the sheep, what is our obligation to fellow sheep in the fold of salvation?

For Prayer:

- Take a moment to pray for the "thieves" and "robbers' who have entered the church of our day. Ask God to bring them to himself or remove them from their positions of authority.

- Ask God to give you a deeper understanding of his voice.

- Ask him to lead you into the richer pastures of the abundant life.

- Thank God that he brought you into the fold. Thank him that he was willing to lay down his life for you as his sheep.

28

Chosen Sheep

Read John 10:22–42

I t was the celebration of the Feast of Dedication. This feast commemorated the rededication of the temple after many years of abandonment. This celebration is known today by Jews as Hanukkah. It is celebrated around the Christmas season. Jesus was in Jerusalem during this feast.

On this occasion, the Jews challenged Jesus: "If you are the Christ, tell us plainly" (verse 24). They were searching for a means of accusing him. "I did tell you, but you do not believe. The miracles I do in my Father's name speak for me," responded Jesus (verse 25). Though they had seen these miracles, the Jews rejected them as a sign of God's approval on Jesus' life and ministry. Jesus told these leaders, who had rejected him, that they did not believe because they were not his sheep (verse 26). The Lord returned to the illustration of the shepherd calling out to the sheep in his fold. On hearing the shepherd's call, the sheep come immediately to follow their shepherd. Those who belong to Christ will hear his voice and follow him. The Jewish leaders could not recognize his voice because they were not his sheep.

This is a hard doctrine for many people to accept. We would all like to believe that we are God's children. This is not so. From the very beginning of time, God has always had a chosen people. He chose the Israelites from among all other nations on the earth to be his people. He revealed himself to them, and they heard his voice. He also has a people today. Those who belong to him will hear his voice and accept him as their Lord and Savior. He came for them. He calls them by name. They respond because they have been given the ability to recognize his voice. Were it not for the fact that the Spirit of God opened my ears and gave me understanding, I would never have been able to understand the wonderful message of the Gospel. I owe my salvation completely to God and his grace in giving me ears to hear and a mind to understand.

The Jews of Jesus' day had heard the Lord speak to them. They saw his miracles. They heard his teaching, but they turned their backs on him. The presence of the Christ himself standing in their midst could not soften their hearts. Perhaps we need to be reminded that this too would be our condition if the Lord Jesus had not removed our old heart of stone and replaced it with a new heart of flesh.

God could have saved every human being that ever walked on the face of this earth—but he didn't. Hell is a reality. Millions of individuals will one day find themselves engulfed in its flames. Why have I escaped these flames, whereas, my neighbor has not? Is it because I am better than my neighbor? Is it because I am more intelligent? Is it because I have a more natural inclination toward the things of God? I am no different from my neighbor. I have escaped the flames of hell only because the Lord Jesus reached out his hand, touched my life, and forgave my sin. Why he chose to touch me and save me and not my neighbor, I may never know. I can only thank him that he did and pray that he will do the same for my neighbor.

Because I am the Lord's sheep, I have heard his voice. I am also secure in him. He has given me eternal life. No one can take that life away from me (verse 28). My Shepherd is greater that any problem or obstacle I will ever encounter. He is greater than any demon of hell or any temptation I will ever face in my lifetime. He is even greater than my own sinful nature. He can overrule my own personal decisions when they are not in my spiritual best interest. He is a good Shepherd. He will not allow me to be overcome by my enemy. Jesus will keep to the end all whom the Father gave him (verse 28). He and his Father are one in this matter.

When the Jewish leaders heard what Jesus said, they picked up stones to stone him. He had claimed to be one with the Father. He claimed to be God. "I have shown you many great miracles from the Father. For which of these do you stone me?" asked Jesus (verse 32). "'We are not stoning you for any of these,' replied the Jews, 'but for blasphemy, because you, a mere man, claim to be God'" (verse 33).

In answer to their accusations, Jesus called their attention to Psalm 82:6. In this Psalm, Asaph, speaking of the political leaders of his day, called them "gods." They were gods because they exercised dominion and authority over the earth. Though they were mere men, the writer of this Psalm, under the inspiration of God, called them "gods." Jesus knew that the Jews had a high regard for the Scriptures. The point Jesus was making was this: if the Psalmist, under the inspiration of God, calls mere men, "gods," how much more does the one sent from God have the right to call himself God's Son?

Before leaving them, Jesus pointed the leaders again to his miracles. He reminded them that the miracles were tangible proof that he was from God. Only God could do the things Jesus did. Though they had heard his reasoning and seen his miracles, the Jews still rejected the Lord Jesus. They tried to seize him by force, but he escaped from them.

Possibly because of their unbelief, Jesus left them and went to the other side of the Jordan River. Here the people believed in his name. What a contrast we have here in these two groups of people. One group could not believe in him. The other group could not help but believe in him. No amount of reasoning or any miracle would ever convince the Jewish leaders that Jesus was the Son of God. Except for the grace of God, you and I would be just like those Jews. If you know the Lord today, thank him that he has given you ears to hear and a mind to understand.

For Consideration:

* How did you come to know the Lord Jesus? What evidence was there that this was the Lord's work?

* What was it that convinced you that Jesus was everything he said he was?

* What kind of relationship exists between the shepherd and his sheep here in this section? What comfort do you take from this?

For Prayer:

* Thank the Lord that he revealed himself to you.

* Ask the Holy Spirit to continue this work of convincing people of the truth in our day.

* Ask God to open the hearts of your loved ones so that they can hear and understand what he is saying.

29

Walking in the Light

Read John 11:1–16

As Jesus ministered on the other side of the Jordan, word came to him that Lazarus was sick. Lazarus had two sisters by the names of Mary and Martha. Mary became known for pouring the bottle of perfume over the feet of Jesus and wiping his feet with her hair (John 12).

Mary and Martha sent for Jesus telling him: "Lord, the one you love is sick" (verse 3). This statement says something about the relationship between Lazarus and Jesus. While this is the first time we read about Lazarus, it is obvious that he knew Jesus very well. Jesus loved Lazarus. They had a close relationship. Notice here that Mary and Martha felt no obligation to mention the name of Lazarus. They simply called him "the one you love." That was sufficient. No name was required. Mary and Martha approached Jesus on this basis. They believed that Jesus would take care of Lazarus, simply because he loved him. We too can come to Jesus on this basis.

In John 9:3 Jesus had told his disciples that the blind man was blind in order that God's glory could be displayed in his life. Jesus repeated this thought in verse 4 of this chapter: "When he heard this, Jesus said, 'This sickness will not end in death. No, it is for God's glory so that God's Son may be glorified through it'" (verse 4).

There is a problem that immediately comes up in this verse. Jesus told his disciples that the sickness of Lazarus would not end in death. As the story unfolds, however, we see that Lazarus did die. How do we reconcile what Jesus said here with what really happened? It is clear that Lazarus did die. He not only died but was wrapped in grave clothes and was put in the tomb. The death of Lazarus, however, was not meant to be permanent. God had not yet finished with him. It was not his God's intention to take him home to be with him at that time. God wanted to raise him from the dead to demonstrate to those who would hear of it that his Son had power over death.

Notice here in verse 5 that although Jesus loved this family, he stayed two more days before coming to see them. These two days were critical for Lazarus. He would die while the Lord waited on the other side of the Jordan. Jesus knew this would happen. Though Jesus loved them, he allowed this family to go through the pain of death.

Jesus was looking at the larger picture. He was looking at the glory of God being revealed through this family. He saw how this tragedy would draw the family closer to each other and to their heavenly Father. Pain is sometimes a necessary ingredient in true love. Do not doubt the love of the heavenly Father for you in your grief. He sees what you do not see. He sees the larger picture. He will work all things out for good. He has your interest in mind.

After two days the Lord told his disciples that they were going to return to Judea. The disciples encouraged him to change his mind. They reminded him that only recently the Jews had tried to stone him in Judea. Listen to Jesus' response to his disciples: "Are there not twelve hours of daylight? A man who walks by day will not stumble, for he sees by this world's light. It is when he walks by night that he stumbles, for he has no light" (verses 9–10).

What was Jesus telling his disciples? First, we need to see here that God has allotted a certain amount of time for each of us to serve him. Jesus had already told his disciples: "As long as it is day, we must do the work of him who sent me. Night is coming, when no one can work" (John 9:4). There is a time limit given to each of us to accomplish the will of God. This time, like the day, does not last forever. This time will one day be cut short by death or some other obstacle.

Second, Jesus was telling his disciples that if he walked in the light, he did not need to fear the obstacles along the way. The safest place to be is in the light of the Father's will and purpose. Jesus told his disciples here that as long as he was doing the will of the Father, he had nothing to fear. It is safer to be in the will of the Father, though af iction and persecution surround us, than to be in the deceptive calm of our own will. Jesus did not need to fear the Jews because it was the will of the Father for him to go to Judea. As long as he was walking in the light of the will of the Father, he would be safe. Are we using the time the Lord has given us to walk in the light of his will? May the Lord find us walking in the light and accomplishing his purposes in the time he has allotted us.

Jesus did not hesitate to go into the very center of hostility. He knew that he would be safe as long as he walked in the light of his Father's will. No one could take his life from him before his time. He encouraged the disciples to follow him. There were blessing awaiting them. They would only know these blessing as they stepped out in faith.

To clarify the reason he was going to Judea, Jesus told

his disciples: "Our friend Lazarus has fallen asleep; but I am going there to wake him up" (verse 11). The disciples didn't quite understand what Jesus was telling them. They thought he was speaking about literal sleep. They had heard that Lazarus was sick. They felt that if he was sick, it would be better for him to get his rest. There was no purpose in risking their lives to wake him from a sleep that would ultimately help him get better. Jesus was not speaking about literal sleep. He clarified things for his disciples by telling them plainly that Lazarus was dead (verse 14).

Notice what Jesus said about the death of Lazarus: "And for your sake I am glad I was not there, so that you may believe" (verse 15). There was a recognition of the fact that God's glory would be revealed in this situation. The death of this saint was in God's perfect plan. A gracious and sovereign God was unfolding his purposes for the good of his people.

Seeing that Jesus had made up his mind about going to Judea, Thomas said: "Let us also go, that we may die with him" (verse 16). His attitude was fatalistic. If we must die, we must die. If this is our lot in life, we must face it. He failed to see the unfolding of the purposes of God in this situation.

Fate tells us that events unfold without any particular reason. The Bible tells us that behind every event in life is a sovereign and personal God. The Creator has skillfully planned and will use everything that happens to each of us. Nothing happens by chance. Even the death of Lazarus had a purpose. As we face the trials and tribulations of life, let us be reminded that it is not fate that determines our course—it is a sovereign and loving God.

While it is yet day, while we still have time, let us commit ourselves to walking in and fully accepting the will of the Father for our lives. Though we do not fully understand now why things happen, we can be assured that as we walk in the light of the Father's perfect will, we will be secure.

For Consideration:

- Have you had times when you saw the Lord taking what appeared to be a tragic circumstance and changing it into something good?

- Have you ever resisted the will of the Father because, like the disciples, you were afraid of what lay ahead? What does this passage have to say about this?

- What is the will of the Father for your life? What gifts and talents has he given you? What burden has he put on your heart? Are you being faithful in this?

For Prayer:

- Thank the Lord for the security we have in him.

- Ask the Lord for courage to face the opposition as you step out to face his will.

- Ask the Lord to help you to use the time he has given you to accomplish his purpose.

- Thank the Lord that he is a sovereign God who works out all things for our good and his glory.

30

The Resurrection of Lazarus

Read John 11:17–57

Jesus had just arrived in Bethany. He had been asked to come because of the sickness of his dear friend Lazarus. Jesus had delayed his departure by two days. By the time he had arrived in Bethany, Lazarus had been in the grave four days. Mary and Martha, his sisters, were in mourning. Many people had come to comfort them.

When Martha heard that the Lord Jesus had arrived, she ran out to meet him. Martha was a person of action. In John 12 we find her busy serving the Lord, while Mary and Lazarus sat at his feet listening to him teach. If there was a job to be done, Martha was the one to do it. Mary, on the other hand, stayed with the people who had come to comfort her. When Martha saw the Lord Jesus, she said to him: "If you had been here, my brother would not have died. But I know that even now God will give you whatever you ask" (verses 21–22).

What is Martha really saying here? Is there, in these

words, a gentle rebuke directed towards Jesus? Is Martha saying, "Lord if only you had come, Lazarus would not have died"? Why had Jesus allowed her brother to die? Why had Jesus taken so long to come? No doubt she had many questions in her mind. Notice, however, that though Lazarus had died, Martha still trusted Jesus: "I know that even now God will give you whatever you ask" (verse 22).

Jesus told Martha that her brother would rise again (verse 23). Martha agreed with Jesus: "I know he will rise again in the resurrection at the last day" (verse 24). She believed that Jesus was trying to comfort her by reminding her that the day would come when she would see Lazarus again in heaven.

This was not what Jesus was telling Martha. He reminded her that he had the power of life in his hands: "I am the resurrection and the life. He who believes in me will live, even though he dies; and whoever lives and believes in me will never die. Do you believe this?" (verses 25–26).

Martha believed that Jesus was the Christ. She knew that he had, as the Son of God, the power of life in his hands. She did not understand, however, what Jesus was really telling her. She did not expect that Jesus would actually raise Lazarus from the dead at that time. Her belief was wonderful. She believed Jesus to be the Christ. She believed that he had the power of life. She believed that he loved Lazarus. She believed that God would give him anything he asked. The problem was not that she did not believe that Jesus could do anything. The problem was that she really didn't expect him to do something right then. I have often found myself in Martha's shoes.

Jesus called for Mary. When Mary arrived, her initial words to Jesus were similar to Martha's: "Lord, if you had been here, my brother would not have died" (verse 32). As she said this, her grief was obvious. Notice the response of

Jesus. He was touched by her grief. He "was deeply moved in spirit and troubled" (verse 33). "Jesus wept" (verse 35).

Why did Jesus weep? Obviously it was not for the same reason as Mary. Mary wept for Lazarus. She would not see him again until the resurrection. Jesus knew that she would see her brother alive and well in just a few short moments. Jesus did not weep for Lazarus. Could it be that he wept for Mary and her grief? While the Lord had allowed her to pass through this grief by delaying his arrival, he still felt her pain. While there was going to be a happy ending to all this pain, Jesus was still deeply moved and troubled in his spirit. Jesus felt what she felt. He identified with her pain and sorrow. He felt the agony of the effects of sin on the earth. Whatever you face today, Jesus also feels that pain with you.

Even the Jews who had come to comfort the family were touched by the grief of Jesus. They too, however, had questions about why Jesus had not come sooner. They wondered why he could not have saved this man from dying when he had opened the eyes of the blind man in Jerusalem.

When all the formalities were over, Jesus brought the people to the tomb. He called for the stone to be rolled away. Martha objected. After four days of decomposition, the body of Lazarus would not have been a pleasant sight. There would have been a horrible odor. Martha was horrified at the thought of seeing the stone rolled away. Jesus reminded her, however, that if she believed, she would see the glory of God. She retracted her objection and waited on him.

It seems that many of us have areas of our lives that we seal up so that no one can enter. Behind these doors there is a foul odor of sin. When the stone is rolled away, the unpleasant odor of impure thoughts, attitudes, and actions rushes out. The Lord stands in front of that stone today and calls for it to be rolled away. Like Martha, we object. We do not want anyone to see what is behind that stone. What victory could be ours if only we were to roll the stone away and let Jesus deal with the corruption behind it. What keeps you today from rolling away that stone and giving Jesus full access to your heart and life?

With the stone rolled away, the Lord called out to Lazarus. Every eye was focused on the place where the body lay. A figure appeared at the doorway. It was bound from head to toe in grave clothes. We can only imagine the shock that rebounded through the crowd that day. Jesus called for the grave clothes to be removed. When they were removed, Lazarus stood before them. He was fully alive. He had been raised from the dead.

What was the response of the people that stood around the tomb that day? Verse 45 tells us that many believed and put their faith in the Lord Jesus. Some of the Pharisees, however, went to their leaders and informed them of what had taken place. The response of the leaders is difficult to imagine: "If we let him go on like this, everyone will believe in him, and then the Romans will come and take away both our place and our nation" (verse 48).

The religious leaders were concerned about two things. First, they were concerned that men and women would believe in the Lord Jesus. To the Pharisees, Jesus was demon-possessed. They did not want people following him. Even the miracle of the raising of Lazarus could not convince them that Jesus was the Son of God. Their second concern was that they would lose their nation. The relationship between the Jews and the Romans was delicate. The Roman authorities would quickly deal with anything that smelled of rebellion. In John 6:15 we see that the people wanted to make Jesus king. If they saw in Jesus their hope of political freedom from the bonds of Rome and attempted to make him king, Rome would be quick to respond. They risked losing their nation.

As they debated this issue among themselves, the high

priest, a man by the name of Caiaphas spoke out: "You know nothing at all! You do not realize that it is better for you that one man die for the people than that the whole nation perish" (verses 49–50).

What was Caiaphas saying here? He was saying that the answer to this dilemma was really quite simple. Jesus was going to have to die. If Jesus didn't die, than the whole nation risked dying by the hands of the Romans. Jesus would have to die to save the nation. What he did not realize at the time was that this statement was prophetic. Jesus would have to die to save the nation. Jesus' death would be their spiritual salvation, however, not their political salvation. From that day forward the Jews decided that Jesus had to die. Orders were given that if anyone found him, they were to report it to the leaders so that Jesus could be arrested (verse 57). After these events, the Lord Jesus withdrew and went to the region of Ephraim with his disciples.

There will always be those who turn their backs on the Lord Jesus. The hearts of the Pharisees were hardened to the cause of Christ. They refused to remove the stone of unbelief and rebellion from their hearts. They would die in their unbelief.

For Consideration:

- What did it take to soften your heart to the things of God?

- Is there a "stone" that needs to be removed in your life? What is it?

- What does this passage teach you about trusting the Lord when things do not turn out as you plan?

For Prayer:

- Ask God to remove the "stones" from your heart.

- Ask God to forgive you for the times you failed to trust in his plan.

- Thank him for the many times he worked things out for good in your life.

31

Mary's Sacrifice

Read John 12:1–11

Some time had passed since Jesus had raised Lazarus from the dead. He had now returned to Bethany were Lazarus lived. A special dinner was given in Jesus' honor. Jesus disciples were also invited.

There were many reasons why such a feast would have been given in the honor of our Lord. Jesus was a close friend of the family. We see this from John 11:3 where Lazarus is referred to as one whom Jesus loved. Also, Jesus had raised Lazarus from the dead. Mary and Martha had lost Lazarus, but Jesus had given him back to them. For that day they were eternally indebted. Beyond these obvious reasons, however, was an even more important reason why Mary, Martha, and Lazarus would give a feast in the honor of Jesus: he had proven to them, beyond a shadow of a doubt, that he was the Son of God.

Jesus is often described as the friend of the poor and needy. This is certainly the case. He showed great compassion toward those who did not have the basic necessities of life. Jesus found in Lazarus, however, a rich friend. Here was a family who could afford to minister to Jesus. This is one of the few times in the Gospel of John where Jesus is being ministered to. Even Jesus, however, needed to be ministered to. Here was just the family that could do it.

The example of the family of Lazarus is a challenge to us. Jesus challenges us in Matthew 10:8: "Freely you have received, freely give." How much Jesus gave to the world, and yet how little he received in return. Maybe there are individuals like this in your circle. These servants are constantly giving of their time, efforts, and resources. Maybe the Lord would have you minister to them.

Martha, as expected, was busy serving the Lord in preparing the meal. Lazarus sat at the table with Jesus. During the meal, Mary brought out a jar of perfume. This was a very expensive perfume. Nard was not found in Israel. It had to be imported into the country. The value of the contents of the jar was estimated at a year's wages. The fact that she had the means to purchase such perfume is an indication of the wealth of the family.

As wealthy as she was, Mary stooped down in front of our Lord. She broke the seal on the jar of perfume and poured the contents over Jesus' feet. With everyone in the room watching, this wealthy woman wiped her Lord's feet with her very own hair.

There are some important details that we do not want to miss in this scene. First, the task of washing feet was left to the servants of the house. It would be inappropriate for the master of the house to stoop down and wash the feet of guests. The second detail we need to see here is that Mary used her hair to dry the Lord's feet. A woman's hair was an object of great pride. Remember what the apostle Paul told the Corinthians: "Does not the very nature of things teach you that if a man has long hair, it is a disgrace to him, but that if a woman has long hair, it is her glory? For long hair is given to her as a covering" (1 Corinthians 11:14–15).

As Mary wiped the dust of her Savior's feet with her hair, she showed him what she felt about him. She was unworthy of washing his feet in the customary way. His feet deserved the very best she had. She washed them with her finest perfume and her hair. Her act shows us that she truly did believe him to be the Son of God.

To the onlookers, this act of devotion was somewhat excessive. Judas, in particular, felt that the money could have been used more wisely by selling the perfume and giving the proceeds to the poor. Jesus disagreed. In verse 7 Jesus told Judas that this perfume had been kept for the express purpose of anointing him for his burial. It is hard to say if Mary had any understanding of the fact that the Lord would soon be crucified. Her action however, symbolized what would soon take place. The Lord would be betrayed, handed over to his enemies, and crucified. Mary's action marked the beginning of the end. Unknown to the disciples around that table, just over one week from then, the Lord would be crucified. This was a very emotional time for Jesus. Mary's anointing reminded him that the end was now very near.

While Jesus was concerned for the poor, no one would see it unfitting to anoint the body of a close friend for death. Her action was acceptable not only because it was offered as a sacrifice to the Son of God but also because she was preparing Jesus for his death. It does not give us the right to be extravagant in the use of our resources and deny the needs of the poor around us, and it does not give us the right to stand in judgment of others who appear to be excessive when we do not understand their motives.

There is one final comment that needs to be made regarding this passage. In verses 9–11 we see that many people began coming to the home of Lazarus. They came not only to see Jesus but also to see Lazarus, whom Jesus had raised from the dead. The resurrection of Lazarus was having a profound effect on the population. Many people believed in Jesus because of this miracle. Lazarus was living proof that Jesus was the Son of God. This did not please the Jewish leaders. They began to make plans to kill Lazarus.

Living for the Lord Jesus is often very costly. We have seen what it meant for Mary to follow the Lord Jesus. We now see what it meant for Lazarus. Every day Lazarus' life would be at risk. As we have already stated, his life was living proof of the truth of the claims of Jesus. How about your life? Is your life a living testimony to the truth of Jesus' claims? If it is, you too risk much for his sake. The enemy has his eye on people like Lazarus.

What does it cost you to be a Christian? Some people are simply in it for the benefits. They take as much as they can get but give little in return. This passage is a challenge to that attitude. Mary gave her best. Lazarus risked his life. What will it mean for you?

For Consideration:

- What sacrifices have you made in becoming a Christian?

- What sacrifices are you willing to make to bring glory to the name of the Lord Jesus?

- What practical lessons do we learn here about judging the actions of others?

- Is your life a practical demonstration of the fact that Jesus is the Son of God?

For Prayer:

- Ask God to make you less judgmental of the actions and attitudes of others.

- Offer yourself and all you have to him again. Ask him to make you willing to sacrifice everything for his glory.

- Ask the Lord to forgive you for the times when you have not given your best to him.

32

Entry into Jerusalem

Read John 12:12–19

The celebration of the Passover was approaching. Jesus knew that this would be the last time he would participate in this great celebration. The Passover looked back to the time when the blood of lambs was placed on the doorposts of the homes of the children of Israel in the land of Egypt (Exodus 12). When the angel of death saw this blood, he passed over their homes and spared their firstborn male children. Any home that did not have the blood sprinkled on the doorposts would lose their firstborn son. The Passover also was a remembrance of how God delivered his people from the bondage of Egypt that same night.

Jesus knew that he would soon become the Passover lamb. His blood would be spilt for the deliverance of his people from the bondage of sin. Mary of Bethany had just anointed Jesus in preparation for this death. One can only imagine the thoughts going through the mind of our Lord as he made his way through the great city of Jerusalem that day.

When the crowd heard that the Lord was on his way to Jerusalem, they gathered palm branches and lined the way that Jesus would travel. As he passed, they waved palm branches to honor him and cried out: "Hosanna! Blessed is he who comes in the name of the Lord! Blessed is the King of Israel!" (verse13).

It is important to examine this statement in more detail. The crowd shouted, "Hosanna," which means "save now." What the crowd shouted that day was, "Save us now." From what did they think they needed to be saved? Obviously, they did not believe it was from their sins. It is more likely that they are asking for political salvation. They were subject to Rome. They wanted freedom. Jesus had proven himself to be able to accomplish great miracles. They believed him to be able to deliver them from the oppression of Rome.

Notice in this statement that they believed Jesus to be the king of Israel. After the feeding of the five thousand, the crowd wanted to make Jesus king, but he would have nothing to do with it. The messiah the crowd was looking for was a political messiah. Their cries were heavy with nationalistic fervor.

Notice the response of Jesus to the cries of the crowd. He found a donkey, mounted him, and rode him the rest of the way into the city. What was the connection between the shouting of the crowd and this action of Jesus?

The crowd claimed him to be a great king who would deliver them from their Roman enemies. The crowd treated him as they would have treated a victorious king returning from war. They lined the way, waving palm branches as symbols of victory.

Christ could have mounted a war horse that day, but he didn't. He chose to mount a donkey. A donkey is an animal used in time of peace. The donkey was used in commerce to transport goods from one place to another. No one would ever mount a donkey to attack the enemy. John is quick to tell us that what Jesus did that day was in fulfillment of the prophecy of Zechariah 9:9–10:

> Rejoice greatly, O Daughter of Zion!
> Shout, Daughter of Jerusalem!
> See, your king comes to you,
> righteous and having salvation,
> gentle and riding on a donkey,
> on a colt, the foal of a donkey.
> I will take away the chariots from Ephraim
> and the war-horses from Jerusalem,
> and the battle bow will be broken.
> He will proclaim peace to the nations.
> His rule will extend from sea to sea
> and from the River to the ends of the earth.

While John only quotes the first part of this prophecy of Zechariah, it is important that we consider the second part as well. Zechariah tells us that the Israel's king would come riding a donkey. When he came, he would come to proclaim peace. The war horse, chariot, and the bow would be taken away from Jerusalem. This king would establish peace with the nations and his dominion would be to the ends of the earth. Jesus rode into Jerusalem on an animal of peace. The crowd cried out for blood. Jesus made it clear that he was seeking peace and not bloodshed. He was not the type of king they were looking for.

The disciples did not understand what Jesus was doing. Later, however, when the Holy Spirit came, they would be reminded of what had taken place that day. Only then would they understand the significance of the Lord's actions that day.

Verses 17 and 18 are also very important to our

understanding of this passage. They tell us the reason why many people had come to see Jesus that day. They had heard of the raising of Lazarus, and they came to see the one who had given him life.

I would like to be more like Lazarus. I would like my life to be such an incredible demonstration of the power of God to change a life that people would line the roads to meet the Savior. I want the work of Christ in me to be of such a nature that people know that it is not me but Christ's power. There is power in a transformed life. Lazarus was a vital testimony to the power of God. People did not stand in awe of Lazarus. They stood in awe of a God who could do such a work in him.

Does this describe your life? Do people see God in you? Do they see the power of a transformed life? Would they line the streets to meet the man who has made such a radical change in your life?

Jesus came into Jerusalem that day riding on a donkey. His purpose was not to be a political ruler. He did not come to rescue his people from the domination of the Roman government. He came to offer peace. He came to transform lives by the power of God. He came to give life. He came to set us free from the bondage and power of evil. His reign was a reign over the hearts and lives of men and women.

For Consideration:

- What evidence is there in your life of the reign and power of the Lord Jesus?

- What keeps you from being a greater witness to the power and love of God?

- How much of God do people see in your life today?

- What false ideas do people have today about the salvation Christ came to offer?

For Prayer:

- Ask God to make you to be a more powerful demonstration of his power and love.

- Thank him that he came to offer peace with God.

- Thank the Lord that he wants to use you to demonstrate his character and power.

33

Surrendered Lives

Read John 12:20–36

T

here were some Greeks among those who lined the roadside to see Jesus as he came into the city of Jerusalem. These Greeks had come to worship at the feast. They approached Philip to ask him if it would be possible to meet Jesus. Philip spoke to Andrew about this. Andrew, in turn, approached Jesus to see if he would like to meet these Greeks. Jesus' response is somewhat perplexing: "The hour has come for the Son of Man to be glorified. I tell you the truth, unless a kernel of wheat falls to the ground and dies, it remains only a single seed. But if it dies, it produces many seeds" (verses 23–24).

When Andrew came to the Lord with the request of the Greeks to see him, Jesus immediately thought about his death. What was it about this request that caused the Lord to speak of his death? To answer this question we must understand that the Jews were the chosen people of God. The door to the Gentile world had not yet been opened.

Salvation came to the Jews first (Romans 1:16). During his ministry, the Lord did not leave the region of Palestine. He worked solely among the Jews. The only way the Greeks could see Jesus would be through his death. The death of Jesus would open the door for the Gentiles to come to him and be forgiven.

To illustrate what he was talking about, the Lord Jesus used the illustration of a grain of wheat. "Unless a kernel of wheat falls to the ground and dies, it remains only a single seed," said Jesus. "But if it dies, it produces many seeds" (verse 24). At this point in history, God was only working with one seed—the seed of Abraham, the nation of Israel. The death of Christ would change that. With the death of Christ (who was of the seed of Abraham), that seed would be multiplied. No longer would the promises of God be centered on one nation. The door for every seed and nation would be opened. Now there are Canadian, African, American, European, and Asian seeds among the chosen people of God. The death of our Lord Jesus opened the door for you and me to become part of his family.

The Greeks who approached Philip only wanted to speak to Jesus; but, Jesus used this incident to teach an important lesson about his death. When he died, the invitation would go out to the Greeks and to every nation on earth to come to see him. The day was coming soon when the salvation of God would be extended to all tribes and nationalities.

Jesus then applied this principle of the seed dying to the lives of all his followers (verse 25). He said: "The man who loves his life will lose it." If you treasure your life so much that you refuse to surrender it to the Lord, you will be sure to wither away spiritually. If you surrender your will to the Lord and let him have control, however, you will have new purpose and produce much fruit. The principle is simple. If you keep your life, you will lose it. If you surrender your life to the Lord, you will find it.

Jesus reminds us that surrendering our lives to him is not always easy. He tells us in verse 26 that whoever wants to serve him must follow him. Remember that Jesus was going to the cross when he said this. If you and I want to serve the Lord Jesus, we must be willing to follow him to the cross. We must not shrink back. To go to the cross is to lose all we treasure. It is to surrender all we have to the Lord Jesus and his cause.

Notice the promise to those who are willing to follow the Lord in this way: "Whoever serves me must follow me; and where I am, my servant also will be. My Father will honor the one who serves me" (verse 26). If we are willing to serve the Lord by following him to the cross, we will dwell with him. Heaven is the reward for those who persevere to the end. There in heaven the Father himself will honor the ones who continued to serve Christ in spite of difficulties. To know that the Father will honor us and that we will dwell eternally with the Son is all the motivation we should need.

It is comforting to know that the Lord Jesus can identify with our fear of complete surrender. In verse 27 the Lord struggled with his coming death. His heart was troubled. "What shall I say?" asked the Lord Jesus, as he looked ahead to his coming death. Should he pray: "Father, save me from this hour"? (verse 27). What would you pray if you were staring a horrible death in the face? Jesus did not pray that the Father would remove this trial. He knew that he had come for this very purpose. Instead he chose to pray: "Father, glorify your name!" (verse 28). This was the heart of the Lord Jesus. He wanted to glorify the name of his Father. His eyes were not on himself but on the Father and the purpose of the Father. What an example this is for us.

Jesus' prayer pleased the Father: "Then a voice came from heaven, 'I have glorified it, and will glory it again'" (verse 29). The life of the Lord Jesus had brought glory to the name of the Father. The Lord's death would bring him that same glory.

The crowd heard the voice of God that day. They were divided about what they heard. Some said it was only thunder. Others believed that an angel had spoken to him. Jesus told them that it was for their benefit that the Father had spoken. It was a confirmation by the Father that what Jesus was about to do, as horrible as it appeared to be, pleased the Father.

In verses 31–32 we are told what the death of Christ would accomplish. First, his death would judge the world. His death sentenced those who would not believe in him to eternal condemnation and separation from God. Second, his death drove out the prince of the world. Satan was defeated the day the Lord Jesus died. The way for sinners to come to God was opened, and Satan could no longer block that way. Satan could do nothing to stop the spread of the gospel and its inevitable results in the lives of men and women coming to faith in the Savior. The third result of the death of Christ would be that all humanity would be drawn to the Savior. Since the crucifixion, the gospel of Christ has spread throughout the entire world. Men and women from every nation have been drawn to the cross of our Lord Jesus and saved from the condemnation of hell. The death of Christ was a turning point in the history of the world. The seed of Abraham, who died on the cross of Calvary, brought life to every nation.

All this talk about the death of Christ caused some doubts in the minds of the crowd that thronged the roadside. This was not what they had anticipated. They had heard that the Messiah would live forever. They had anticipated that he would remain with them and deliver them from the hands of the Romans. Now that he was talking about death, they began to wonder if he really was the Messiah. Knowing their doubts, Jesus reminded the crowd that he was only going to be with them a little longer. He challenged them to turn to him as the light before it was too late (verses 35–36). While he was in their midst, Jesus showed the crowd the way of salvation. Soon he would die and no longer be with them. Now was the time for them to turn to him and walk in the path of salvation. That opportunity might not come again.

For Consideration:

- What holds you back from giving your all to the Lord Jesus today?

- Have you experienced the life that comes from death to self? What blessings have you received from the Lord as a result of surrendering to him and his will for your life?

- Have you ever found yourself asking the Lord to remove all your struggles? What do we learn from the prayer of Jesus here about suffering?

For Prayer:

- Thank the Lord that through his death he opened the door for us to come to him.

- Ask him to make you willing to surrender all to him.

- Ask him to give you courage to face the trials that come your way. Ask him to glorify his name in you through the trials he allows you to face.

34

Blinded by God

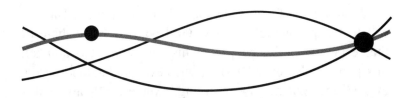

Read John 12:37–50

Anyone whose mind was open to examining objectively what they saw in the miracles of Jesus would have to come to the conclusion that he was no mere man. Jesus' power went far beyond the power of a mere man. The recent resurrection of Lazarus from the dead proved beyond a shadow of a doubt that the Lord Jesus had at his disposal the power of life itself.

John 12:37 tells us that although they had seen these great miracles, most of the people of Jesus' day refused to believe in him. It seems incredible that Jesus, the Son of God, could have walked in their midst and shown them his power and glory, and yet they refused to believe. How could they have been so blind?

To explain this blindness, John quoted Isaiah the prophet: "Lord, who has believed our message and to whom has the arm of the Lord been revealed?" (verse 38). You can almost sense the prophet's frustration in these words. The rejection of the things of God is not a recent problem. Men and women from the time of Adam have turned their backs on the Lord. Why is this? John gives us an answer in verse 40, continuing to quote from Isaiah: "He has blinded their eyes and deadened their hearts, so they can neither see with their eyes, nor understand with their hearts, nor turn—and I would heal them." Isaiah tells us that the Lord blinded their eyes and deadened their hearts so they could not see. We need to examine this difficult verse in more detail.

John's quote from Isaiah came in the context of Isaiah's call to the prophetic ministry. God warned Isaiah here of the response of the people to his ministry: "Go and tell this people: 'Be ever hearing, but never understanding; be ever seeing, but never perceiving.' Make the heart of this people calloused; make their ears dull and close their eyes. Otherwise they might see with their eyes, hear with their ears, understand with their hearts, and turn and be healed" (Isaiah 6:9–10).

At first glance it appears that the Lord was calling the prophet to go to his people in order to harden their hearts. We need to understand, however, that the Lord God sees what we cannot see. He sees the end from the beginning. He sent Isaiah to preach a message of repentance to his people. He sent Isaiah to proclaim his Word to a people who had wandered far from the truth. God wanted them to return to him. That was why he sent Isaiah. God knew, however, what the result of the preaching of Isaiah would be. He knew that the people would turn their backs on him. He knew that they would reject the message of his prophet. He knew that the people would harden their hearts. Though he knew in advance what their response would be, he still gave them a chance to repent, by sending his servant.

When God told Isaiah to go and make the hearts of the people calloused, their ears dull, and their eyes closed, he was speaking as one who knew what the result of the preaching of Isaiah would be. God sends us to all people, regardless of whether they respond favorably to our message or not. God knows those who will respond and those who will refuse, but he still sends us to them all.

Not everyone was blind who listened to the Lord Jesus that day. There were some who did believe in him. Notice, however, that they did not confess their faith in him because they feared the Jews (verse 42). They did not want to face the possibility of being cast out of the synagogue and become publicly disgraced, "for they loved the praise from men more than praise from God" (verse 43). This problem is not unique to the people of Jerusalem in Jesus' day—we still wrestle with it today.

John concluded this section of Scripture with a reaffirmation of Jesus' divine nature. He reminds us that it is impossible to believe in Jesus only. To believe in Jesus is also to believe in the one who sent him (verses 44–45). John tells us that we cannot truly believe in Jesus if we do not also believe in his Father. To look at Jesus is to see the Father in him. Jesus is the perfect representation of the Father. All he did and said re ected the character of his Father. This is why Jesus could say in John 14:9: "Anyone who has seen me has seen the Father."

The union between Jesus and the Father is such that the words the Lord Jesus spoke are the words of the Father himself. To reject the words of Christ is to reject the words of the Father and to bring judgment on oneself (verses 48–50). Because the very words Jesus spoke here were the words of the heavenly Father, we must take them seriously. We must listen and obey them. These words bring either life or condemnation. The Jews of Jesus' day so hardened their hearts that they could no longer hear what God had to say to them. By rejecting the words Jesus spoke, they also rejected the Father. Those who heard Jesus that day failed to understand this truth. They sealed their judgment. They had hardened their hearts and rejected the Son of God.

For Consideration:

- Have you ever found yourself resisting the Word of God and his will for your life? Where did that lead you?

- What is it that causes this resistance in your life? What stands between you and the acceptance of God's will for your life?

- Have you ever found yourself doubting the promises of the Word of God? What keeps you from stepping out boldly in those promises?

For Prayer:

- Ask God to give you a heart that is soft to his Word.

- Have you been resisting the call of God in your life? Take a moment to confess your sin and surrender right now to his will.

- Do you have a friend or loved ones who have been resisting the Lord? Ask the Lord to soften their hearts today.

35

Jesus Washes the Disciples' Feet

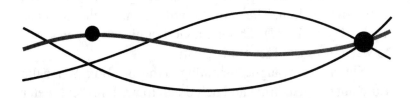

Read John 13:1–17

It was just before the Passover. Unknown to the disciples, this would be the last time they would celebrate this feast with Jesus. Soon he would be arrested and handed over to be crucified. Jesus and his disciples were together for a meal. When the meal was over, the Lord Jesus took a towel and basin and, kneeling down before the disciples, proceeded to wash their feet.

There are two important facts mentioned in verses 2–4 that help us understand the full impact of what was happening here. The first of these facts concerns Judas Iscariot. Verse 2 tells us that the devil had already put it in the heart of Judas to betray the Lord. While this fact was hidden from the other disciples, it was not hidden from our Lord. He knew that Judas would betray him. Jesus bent down to wash the feet of his betrayer. It is relatively easy to do good to those who do good to us. It is not so easy to do good to our enemies. This is what Jesus was doing here.

The second important fact for our consideration is found in verse 3. This verse tells us that Jesus knew that the Father had put all things into his hands. He knew that he had come from God and was going to God. What does this tell us? It tells us that the Lord Jesus is God. God the Father had placed all things into his hands. The destiny of the world was laid on the shoulders of the Lord Jesus. The Father placed full confidence in him. The person who stooped down in front of the disciples was the Lord of all. He holds our destiny in his hands. There is none greater than he. Kings of the earth will bow down to him. The earth trembles at his sight (Romans 14:11; Psalm 114:7). This great God of glory stooped down to wash the dusty feet of his creatures.

Simon Peter caught something of this paradox. When the Lord approached him and knelt down to wash his feet, Peter wanted nothing to do with it. Was it because Peter had too much respect for his master? Did he feel that it was below the dignity of his Lord to stoop down to wash his feet? Jesus' response to Peter was astounding: "Unless I wash you, you have no part of me" (verse 8). Jesus, in his typical style, spoke of spiritual things. The washing of the feet was a symbol of the washing that must take place in the lives of all believers. It was symbolic of the ultimate humiliation of our Lord Jesus, his death on the cross.

What the Lord was saying to Peter that day was something like this, "Peter if you do not let me humble myself for you, you cannot be part of me. It is necessary that I humble myself before you so that you can become clean. It is necessary that I die so that you may be forgiven of your sins. If I do not cleanse you of your sins, you cannot be my child. If I do not wash you, you will have no part of me."

"'Then, Lord,' Simon Peter replied, 'not just my feet but my hands and my head as well!'" (verse 9). If Peter was going to do something, he was going to do it with all his heart. (This often got Peter in trouble.) Jesus answered Peter:

"A person who has had a bath needs only to wash his feet" (verse 10).

Imagine an individual who, after having a bath, walked to his friend's house on the dusty Jerusalem roads. When he arrived, he discovered that his feet were dirty. Did he, for the sake of his dusty feet, need to have another bath? No, all that was required was that he wash his feet and he would be clean again.

There seems to be a hidden spiritual meaning in this statement of Jesus. He told his disciples that they were all clean except one of them who would betray him (verses 10–11). The cleanliness that Jesus was referring to here was the cleansing of their souls. All except Judas believed in Jesus and wanted to walk in his light. Peter, like the other disciples, had been washed by Christ. His sins had been forgiven and his salvation assured.

As believers, who had been washed in the blood of the Lamb of God, these disciples still lived in a sinful world. As they walked on the dusty, sinful soil of this earth, they would become dirty. They would often require a spiritual foot-washing. You and I know how much we are influenced by the things of this world. None of us can walk through this life without being stained by the dirt and filth of this world. We struggle with temptations. We fall short of the standard that the Lord has laid out for us. Like a weary traveler on the dusty Jerusalem roads, we too must make it a habit to come to the Lord for a regular spiritual foot-washing. We must bring to him our sins and out shortcomings and have him cleanse us regularly.

Jesus was telling Peter that he had already been forgiven. He was clean. His relationship with the Lord was established. Jesus reminded him, however, that he would have to come back to him regularly for further cleansing and forgiveness. Could it be that Jesus was thinking here about Peter's denial of the Lord at the time of his trial? God would not forsake him on that day. Peter would, however, have to come to him for forgiveness and cleansing for the denial of his Lord.

Our spiritual bath is a once-for-all experience. We receive the Lord and are cleansed from our sin. We know the forgiveness of God. This does not mean that we will never fall into sin again. We will need to come daily for a spiritual foot-washing. We must learn to live in the cleansing that the Lord provides. The fact that we have sinned does not mean that we have lost our salvation. When we fall short, we must return to Jesus for forgiveness and restoration.

Having washed their feet, Jesus encouraged his disciples to follow his example (verse 15). Jesus was not necessarily instituting the practice of foot-washing in the church (though it might do us all good to experience such a ceremony). There are many ways of washing one another's feet. Ultimately, to wash each other's feet is to serve one another as Christ served us. It is to forgive one another as Christ has forgiven us. Notice that Jesus was not telling his disciples that it would be a nice thing for them to serve each other in this way. He was telling them that, if they wanted to follow him, they would *have to serve* each other in this way. Not to do so would be to disobey the clear teaching of Scripture.

If the Master of the universe stooped down to wash the feet of his disciples, we too must be willing to stoop down and serve our brothers and sisters in their need. "Now that you know these things, you will be blessed if you do them" (verse 17).

For Consideration:

• Is it possible to live the Christian life without sinning?

• Are there any sins that you need to confess before the Lord today?

- Notice how willing Jesus was to wash the feet of his disciples. What hinders you from approaching him today with your need of cleansing?

- Are you willing to wash the feet of a "Judas" in your life? Do you have people who have been seeking your harm? How can you bless them today?

- Are there individuals you need to reach out to in the name of Christ, as Jesus did that day? Who are they? What would Christ have you do for them?

For Prayer:

- Ask the Lord to reveal any hidden sin to you that needs to be confessed. Come to him for a "spiritual foot-washing."

- Thank him for the cleansing he provides.

- Ask God to open your eyes to the needs around you. Ask him to give you more of the attitude of Christ.

36

Betrayed

Read John 13:18–38

Have you ever been shocked by the news that you have been betrayed by someone you love? Betrayal is never easy. When it comes from someone who is close to you, it is very difficult. Jesus had hand-picked his twelve disciples. They had lived and worked together for almost three years. Relationships had formed among them. They had laughed together and cried together. In the last few years, they had seen wonderful things together. They were a real team. On this particular occasion, Jesus and his twelve disciples were together. After the meal, Jesus had taken a towel and washed the disciples' feet. When he finished, he made a shocking announcement: "He who shares my bread has lifted up his heel against me" (verse 18).

We can only imagine the shock of those words. What does it mean "to lift up one's heel" against someone else? This phrase may be a reference to a horse that lifts up its heel to kick. "To lift up one's heel" means "to seek to harm."

What Jesus was saying here was that there was someone in the room who was a traitor. Notice that the heel was not being lifted up against the disciples. Jesus was the focus of its attention.

What made this statement all the more shocking was that Jesus told his disciples that the person who would lift up his heel ate bread with them. We eat bread with people we trust. This would make the act of betrayal even more hideous. The person who betrayed Jesus was a friend.

In verse 19 John tells us that Jesus wanted his disciples to know about this act of betrayal before it happened so that "when it does happen you will believe that I am He." The "He" in this passage was the Messiah who was to come to save them from their sins. Jesus was soon going to die. The disciples would be challenged in their faith at his death. Jesus wanted his disciples to know beforehand that he would be betrayed and led to the cross of Calvary, so they would not lose hope when he was crucified.

While the death of the Lord Jesus would be very difficult for the disciples to understand, they would eventually come to understand the hope that this death brought. These very disciples would go to the far corners of the earth with the message of Christ, the crucified and risen Messiah. Jesus promised that those who accepted them and their message also accepted him (verse 20). While the devil meant the betrayal to hinder the cause of the Kingdom by killing the Lord Jesus, his death would instead become its central message. Men and women throughout all ages would be set free from the power of evil through this powerful message of salvation.

Verse 21 tells us that the thought of this betrayal and death troubled Jesus. "One of you is going to betray me," he told them. He knew this from the beginning, but it did not make it any easier when the day approached. The disciples did not know what to think. They looked around the room, wondering who he was speaking about. Simon Peter asked "the disciple whom Jesus loved" (John) to ask Jesus for the name of this betrayer (verses 23–24). Jesus told them that it was the one to whom he would offer the bread dipped in the dish (verse 26).

In Bible times eating utensils were relatively unknown. Often the meal would be brought to the table in a bowl. Bread was served with the meal and was usually dipped into the dish of broth or meat. When the host dipped bread in the dish and offered it to a guest, he was showing particular favor to that guest. Jesus showed this favor to Judas, despite the fact that he would shortly betray him. Jesus treated Judas with respect and honor.

Jesus dipped the bread in the dish and offered it to Judas. Had Judas heard what Jesus had just said about the betrayer eating the bread dipped in the dish? If he heard what Jesus said, by accepting this bread, he was accepting his role as a traitor. From John 13:2 we understand that the devil had already put it into the heart of Judas to betray the Lord. When Judas took the bread, however, Satan entered him (verse 27). Judas, by accepting this gesture of friendship, accepted becoming the instrument of Satan to betray the Lord. This was a conscious choice on the part of Judas. Satan entered him only when he had willingly become his instrument.

Notice that after Satan entered into him, Judas could not remain in the presence of Jesus. The passage tells us that Judas left. He was no longer comfortable in the presence of Jesus and the disciples. Light has no fellowship with darkness. (See 2 Corinthians 6:14.) Satan has no fellowship with Christ. To make a conscious choice to betray the Lord is to cut oneself off from fellowship with him. The disciples did not understand why Judas left. They thought he had some business to take care of.

Knowing that the wheels were now in motion for his betrayal and crucifixion, the Lord told his disciples: "Now is the Son of Man glorified" (verse 31). The glorification of the Lord Jesus would come by means of his death and resurrection. He reminded his disciples here that he would not be with them much longer. This would have been difficult for the disciples to understand.

Before he left them, the Lord Jesus told his disciples that his great desire for them was that they love one another (verse 34). He reminded them that the world would know that they were his disciples if they loved one another. The Lord had just been speaking in this passage of how he loved his disciples. He was ready to go to the cross for them. This is the example he sets for us. Can we love one another that much? Are we willing to die to ourselves for the cause of our loved ones and enemies? Jesus was reminding his disciples that, if they loved one another in this way, they would prove to the world that the love of God lived in them and that they were truly his disciples.

There is an important truth in this new command. John would later amplify what Jesus said here in his first epistle. Listen to what John later wrote:

> We know that we have passed from death to life, because we love our brothers. Anyone who does not love remains in death. Anyone who hates his brother is a murderer, and you know that no murderer has eternal life in him. This is how we know what love is: Jesus Christ laid down his life for us. And we ought to lay down our lives for our brothers. If anyone has material possessions and sees his brother in need but has no pity on him, how can the love of God be in him? Dear children, let us not love with words or tongue but with actions and in truth. (1 John 3:14–18)

The proof that we are the children of God is in the love of God that dwells in our hearts.

As Peter listened to what the Lord was telling them that day, he was grieved in his heart. He was not ready for the Lord to die. He told the Lord that he was willing to follow him wherever he went. He was even willing to lay down his life for him. "Will you really lay down thy life for me?" Jesus asked Peter. "Before the rooster crows, you will disown me three times!" (verse 38). This would have been very difficult for Peter to understand.

Peter's denial causes us to re ect very deeply on our own relationship with Christ. The apostle Paul tells us that it is a dangerous thing to overestimate our strength to stand firm for the Lord: "So, if you think you are standing firm, be careful that you don't fall!" (1 Corinthians 10:12).

Peter felt sure of his relationship with the Lord, but he fell at on his face. A chain is only as strong as its weakest link. You may be strong in many areas of your life, but you have one weak link. As Satan pulls with all his might on the chain of your spiritual consecration to the Lord Jesus, it really does not matter how strong all the other links are. Just one weak link can cause your chain to break. You cannot afford to have even one weak link in your chain.

Judas made a conscious decision to betray our Lord. Peter fell because of a weak link in his chain. Both men were disciples. Both of them fell. This reminds us that we too need to be on our guard. Peter, as an old man, looking back over his life (and possibly thinking about his own denial of the Lord) brings this challenge to us: "Be self-controlled and alert. Your enemy the devil prowls around like a roaring lion looking for someone to devour" (1 Peter 5:8). We can become so confident in our relationship with the Lord that we let down our guard. Always be on the alert. The battle is not over yet.

For Consideration:

- Have there been times in your life when you have become suddenly aware of your weaknesses?

- What are some of the weak links in the chain of your commitment to the Lord Jesus?

- What does it take to remain strong and faithful in your walk with God?

For Prayer:

- Has someone you love ever betrayed you? Ask the Lord to heal the hurt of this betrayal.

- Ask God to show you the weak links in the chain of your commitment to him. Ask him to strengthen those weak links.

- Ask the Lord to help you realize how much you really do need him if you are going to be able to conquer the enemy.

- Do you know some people who have fallen in their walks with the Lord God? Ask the Lord to minister to them and bring them back to himself. Ask him to show you if there is anything he would have you do to minister to them.

37

I Am the Way

Read John 14:1–6

It would not be difficult for us to imagine what the atmosphere was like in the room. Jesus had just told the disciples that one of them would betray him. This little group had worked together for three years. They had learned to live with and respect one another during this time. To discover that one of them would betray the Lord Jesus was difficult to believe. To betray Jesus was to betray the friendships that they had been built over these last few years.

The disciples had been astonished at this prophetic statement of Jesus (13:22). In his pride Peter had told Jesus that he was willing to lay down his life for him (13:37). Jesus had told Peter, however, that he would instead deny him three times. No doubt Peter would have had a hard time imagining this.

Added to all this talk about betrayal and denials, Jesus had told his disciples that he was going to die (13:36). The disciples loved their master. They had left everything to follow him. Their lives for three years had revolved around the Lord Jesus. They were nothing without him. This talk of his death would have been unnerving for them to consider.

Jesus felt the atmosphere of that evening: "Do not let your hearts be troubled. Trust in God; trust also in me" (verse 1). The disciples were about to lose someone they had given their lives to serve. Jesus felt their fears and pain and challenged them to put their trust and confidence in God. No matter how dismal the situation might become, almighty God was still worthy of their confidence. Nothing that was about to happen would be out of his control. Judas would let them down. Peter would let them down. God, however, would always be there for them. God would prove faithful to them in their trials. What a comfort this ought to be for us as well.

Jesus continued to encourage his disciples by telling them why he was going to leave them. He told them that he was going to prepare a place for them (verse 2). "I will come back and take you to be with me that you also may be where I am" (verse 3). He would only be gone temporarily. He promised to return to take them to be with him. There was a bright future waiting for them.

Thomas, in particular, seemed to be confused: "Lord, we don't know where you are going, so how can we know the way?" (verse 5). To this, Jesus answered: "I am the way and the truth and the life. No one comes to the Father except through me" (verse 6). In this statement, Jesus told Thomas where he was going and how to get there. He told him first that he was going to the Father ("no one comes to the Father"). This statement tells us that this was where Jesus was going. Secondly, Jesus told Thomas that he was the way to the Father.

Let's consider this in a little more detail. How can I get to heaven through Jesus? The one thing that keeps us from heaven is our sin. The only way that you or I can be saved from the condemnation of God is by being forgiven for our sin. God would not be just if he ignored sin. A judge who pardoned crime because he did not have the heart to condemn a criminal would not be a good judge. Sin must be punished. The criminal cannot be allowed to roam the streets without paying for his or her crimes. Jesus chose to take the penalty for our sin on himself. He died on our behalf. He paid the debt we owed but could not pay. Because of Christ, all is forgiven for those who believe. The obstacle of our sin is removed.

There is no way that we can pay the penalty for our sin. Jesus alone could pay the price. By his death on the cross of Calvary, he has paid that price. We simply need to open our hearts and receive what the Lord so richly offers. The way to heaven is open for those who accept Christ's payment for their sin. While the disciples wrestled with this concept at that time, its truth would radically impact their lives and ministries.

The truth is incredibly simple. Jesus is the way to the Father. He removed the infinite debt of sin that we owed to the Father. All we need to do now is come to Jesus and accept what he has done for us. There can be nothing simpler. There can be nothing more life-changing.

For Consideration:

- What things do people trust in to get to heaven? What does this passage tell us about the foolishness of trusting in these things?

- How is Jesus the way to the Father?

- What did Jesus tell his disciples to do in their fears and pain? How does this apply to us today? What is your pain? How can you apply this truth to your life today?

For Prayer

- Thank the Lord that he has done everything for your salvation.

- Do you know of people who are trusting in something other than the finished work of Christ for their salvation? Ask the Lord to show them the way.

- Thank the Lord that you can come to him in your pain. Thank him that he is willing to reach out to you in these times.

38

Show Us the Father

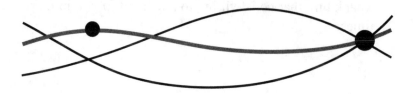

Read John 14:7–31

In John 14:7 Jesus told his disciples that if they knew him, they would know the Father as well. He went as far as to say that they had actually seen the Father. What did Jesus mean by this? The Lord Jesus was the exact image of the Father. When the disciples looked at Jesus and saw his compassion for the lost, they saw the compassion of the Father in him. When they listened to his wisdom, they heard the wisdom of God, for the words he spoke were the words of the Father. When they saw him heal the sick or raise the dead, they saw the power of the Father at work in him. By understanding the character and power of Jesus, we understand the character and power of the Father, for they are one. Christ's human body deceived many, but Jesus was the Son of God.

Philip did not understand what the Lord Jesus was saying here: "Lord, show us the Father and that will be enough for us" (verse 8). What was Philip really saying? There had been a lot of theological talk in those days about the person of the Lord Jesus. Jesus had often told them that he and the Father were one. This was not easy for the disciples to understand. Maybe in one sense Philip was saying something like this, "Lord all this talk is fine, but what we really need is a practical demonstration. Show us the Father and we will understand what you are talking about."

There was a tone of disappointment in the voice of the Lord when he responded to Philip's request: "Don't you know me, Philip, even after I have been among you such a long time? Anyone who has seen me has seen the Father. How can you say, 'Show us the Father'?" (verse 9).

Philip really did not know Jesus. If he had understood what the Lord was saying that day, he would never have asked to see the Father. By seeing Jesus, Philip had also seen the Father. Jesus went on to explain more fully what he meant. He reminded Philip that the Father was in the Son, and the Son was in the Father. The words that Philip heard the Son speak were the words of the Father. The miraculous works that the Son did were not his own works—they were the works of God the Father, who lived in him. When Philip saw these works, he saw the power of God at work in the person of our Lord Jesus.

Jesus told his disciples that this same power could be evident in their lives as well. If they had faith in him, they could do even greater works than he did (verse 12). They could ask anything in his name and it would be done for them. These same disciples would live out the truth of what Jesus was telling them. When they became empowered by the Spirit of God, they too would see the Father's power in their lives. In that power, they would heal the sick. The message of the gospel would spread in power from these disciples to the far corners of the earth. People from every nation would come to know and love the Lord Jesus. All of this was a demonstration of the power of the Father at work in their lives.

We can know the presence and the power of the Father at work in our lives and ministry. Jesus promised in verses 16–17 that he would send the Counselor. This Counselor, according to Jesus, was the Spirit of truth. Though Jesus had to leave his disciples to go to his Father, he would not leave them powerless. The Counselor would dwell in them and teach them all they needed to know (verse 26). The Counselor would bring to their minds all that the Lord had taught them. This is Christ's promise to us as well.

How can we know this power in our lives? Jesus gives us the answer in verse 23: "If anyone loves me, he will obey my teaching. My Father will love him, and we will come to him and make our home with him (verse 23). The secret to knowing the power of God at work in our lives is to love the Lord and to live in obedience to his Word. The promise here is that if we love Christ and live in obedience to his Word, the Lord Jesus will come, by means of his Spirit, and make his home with us. If we want to be filled with God's Spirit and know the power of his presence in our lives, we need to deal with the obstacles that stand in the way. Disobedience and lack of love for God will only hinder the work of the Spirit of God through us. We must set our hearts to love God and to obey him, no matter the cost.

Have you ever seen a river blocked by a branch? As debris oats down this river, it gets caught on the branch. Soon the course of the river is changed and the ow of water is interrupted. How can that ow be restored? The only way to restore the normal ow of the river is to clean out the obstacles. Disobedience, like this branch, is a hindrance to the free owing of God's power in our lives. If we want to know the filling and empowering of the Spirit of God in our lives, we need to learn to be obedient.

Not only did Jesus promise his disciples the power of the Holy Spirit, but he also promised his peace in their lives. The disciples were quite troubled at that time. The peace the Lord would give them would not depend on outward circumstances. This peace could be experienced in the midst of turmoil. It is a peace that comes from knowing that we are right with God. It is a peace that comes from the presence of God in our lives. Nothing can frustrate the plans and purposes of an all-powerful God. Worry and fear are unknown to God. When his Spirit lives in us, we too experience this peace. It comes from knowing God and knowing that he is in perfect control of all the events and circumstances of life. When we are one with God and his Spirit lives in us, we know this peace.

Jesus reminded the disciples that if they loved him, they would be glad that he was leaving to go to his Father (verse 28). Who among us would not delight in going to be with our loving heavenly Father? Jesus was leaving this world of sin and going to be in the presence of his Father. This was cause for rejoicing.

Jesus told his disciples that his Father was greater than he was (verse 28). This is a difficult statement to understand. If the Son was the perfect re ection of the Father and they were one, how could it be that the Father was greater than he? We need to understand this statement of Jesus by examining the context of this chapter. Jesus was about to die. In verse 31, Jesus told his disciples that he did exactly what the Father asked him to do. Christ voluntarily submitted to doing the will of the Father. He willingly accepted his coming death. It was in this sense that the Father was greater than the Son. The Son, though equal to the Father, humbled himself to do the will of the Father. For a time he became the servant of the Father to accomplish the great plan of redemption for humankind.

Jesus warned his disciples that the prince of this world was coming (verse 30). Satan was about to accomplish his plan to kill Jesus. Jesus reminded his disciple, however, that Satan did not have any hold on him. Satan could not keep him in the grave. Christ's purposes would be accomplished even in his death. God would rule over the evil schemes of the devil to bring about redemption.

Jesus' disciples were saddened that day when they discovered that Jesus was going to leave them to be with his Father. Jesus sought to encourage them here in this passage. He promised that he would send the Holy Spirit to them and fill them with the peace of God. They would also know the power of God in their lives. They would do the works that Jesus had done, and even greater works. He promised them that though they would encounter trials and obstacles on the way, Satan himself would not be able to hinder the purpose and plan of God for their lives.

What wonderful promises were offered to the disciples that day. Peace, power, and victory over Satan himself was all theirs. These same promises are offered to us as well. Have we experienced the reality of these promises?

For Consideration:

- How much of the power and peace of the Lord Jesus is being demonstrated in your life right now?

- What blocks the flow of God's power and peace in your life today?

- To what extent is your life a reflection of the character of God?

- What encouragement do you receive here in this passage regarding your fight with Satan?

For Prayer:

- Ask God to make you an instrument of his power and peace.

- Ask God to reveal to you the obstacles in your life that keep you from being everything he has called you to be. Ask him to forgive you and set you free to minister in his power and with his peace.

- Thank the Lord that he has promised victory over Satan and his demons.

39

The Vine and the Branches

Read John 15:1–8

I n John 15 Jesus paints a picture of a vine and its branches. In this picture, Jesus is the vine. We are the branches. God the Father is the gardener. Let us consider this picture in some detail here.

God the Father, as the gardener, has a deep concern for the branches of the vine, which are his people. Like any good gardener, he carefully examines these branches. He removes the dead and useless ones because they are only a hindrance to the rest of the branches on the vine. He prunes the productive and fruitful branches so they can produce more fruit. The deep desire of the heavenly gardener is for each branch on the vine to produce much fruit. He wants to see them reach their full potential.

While this image is perfectly understandable in the world of gardening, it is more difficult to accept in the spiritual sense. The very nature of people demands that they be pruned from time to time. We have a natural tendency to send up shoots in the wrong directions. We have a natural leaning to become lazy and unprofitable because of our sin. We are all inclined to accept mediocrity in our spiritual lives. To live as God requires demands effort, sacrifice, and pain. Like garden branches, if left alone, we tend to become unfruitful and unproductive for the Lord. It is necessary that the Lord prune the sin that is the cause of this unfruitfulness.

Pruning is not an easy thing for most of us. In pruning us God is removing any obstacle that keeps us from producing all the fruit he desires us to produce. I remember a time in my life when God began this pruning process. He had to break my pride that kept me believing that I could somehow accomplish the work he called me to do in my own strength. He stripped me of my health for a period of months. He took away much of my ministry. He seemed to pull back from me for a time in my spiritual walk, and I was left feeling helpless. This was not an easy time. Even as I write now I am still walking through this time of dryness in my life. These times of pruning are designed to enable us to produce even more fruit. After the pruning, however, we can expect a time of fruitfulness. It is the heart of the Father that we produce fruit. He will do whatever it takes to enable us to be fruitful.

Notice that this vine has many branches that bear no fruit (verse 2). We have all seen vines or trees with dead branches. In the physical world, this illustration does not cause any problem. The problem, however, comes when we seek to understand the deeper spiritual meaning to this parable. We need to examine this illustration in greater detail. Believers interpret this verse in various ways.

There are those who believe that because these fruitless branches are part of the vine, they are believers who have broken communion with God and have died spiritually. Because they are dead, they are cut off the vine. They are no longer part of Christ. They believe that this verse suggests that it is possible, by means of our rebellion, to lose our salvation. This interpretation, however, seems to run contrary to the rest of the teaching of Scripture.

The second suggestion is that the unproductive branches on the vine represent people who, though part of the visible church, do not really belong to the Lord Jesus. There are many individuals attending churches across our nations who do not truly belong to the Lord Jesus. Outwardly, they appear to be part of the vine, but they have no inner relationship with the Lord. We can tell who these individuals are by the fact that they are unproductive in their spiritual lives. They do not produce fruit because they have no spiritual life in them. The day is coming when these individuals will be exposed for who they really are. They will be cut off because they do not belong to Christ.

The final suggestion regarding the identity of these dead branches is that they represent true Christians who have lost their communion with the Lord because of the hardness of their hearts. They are cut off, not from their salvation but rather from intimate communion with the Lord. They have become useless to the Lord and his purposes. They are virtually indistinguishable from the rest of the world.

When Israel turned her back on the Lord, he sent her into exile. God did this because the normal pruning was not sufficient. Israel needed to be purified by fire. The apostle Paul spoke of the fire that unproductive Christians will one day face.

> If any man builds on this foundation using gold, silver, costly stones, wood, hay or straw, his work will be shown for what it is, because the Day will bring it to light. It will be revealed with fire, and the fire will test the quality of each man's work. If what he has built survives, he will receive his reward. If

it is burned up, he will suffer loss; he himself will be saved, but only as one escaping through the ames. (1 Corinthians 3:12–15)

The individuals who face the fire of God's judgment here are children of God. They will be saved "but only as one escaping the ames."

Ezekiel the prophet also used the illustration of the vine (Ezekiel 15). He described the Israelites as a useless vine that was pulled out of the fire. The fire described in John 15 does not necessarily represent the fire of hell. These branches face the fire of God's judgment. Though they are his children, they are judged because of their sin and unfruitfulness.

What we need to see here is the desire of the Father that we produce fruit in our lives. It angers him that believers are not taking advantage of the life of the vine to produce much fruit. It is the business of the vine to produce fruit. This leads us to a very important question: How can I produce this fruit? Jesus gives us the answer in the next few verses.

First, if we want to bear fruit, we must allow the Lord to prune us. In verse 3 the Lord told his disciple that they were clean by means of the word he had spoken to them. We miss the significance of this verse in the translation. The Greek word used to translate the word "prune" in verse 2 can also mean "to clean." To prune is to clean. When the gardener prunes his vine, he is cleaning the vine of all dead and unfruitful branches. The Lord told his disciples that they were pruned by means of the Word. The Lord prunes us by means of his Word. His Word shows us the sin in our lives. His Word gives us direction in life. The Word of God, like a sword, often cuts deeply into the intimate areas of our lives and reveals the sin and rebellion that lurks in the shadows. If we want to be fruitful for the Lord Jesus, we must allow him to prune away the sin of our lives by means of the sword of the Word of God. We cannot expect to be fruitful if we are living in disobedience to the Word of God. We need to allow the Word to prune us.

Second, if we want to be productive for the Lord Jesus we must learn how to remain in him (verse 4). The temptation for every Christian is to wander from the vine. Our natural pride causes us to rush ahead of the Lord and seek to do all we can in our own strength. To remain in the Lord is to live in obedience to his Word. It is to maintain communion with him. It is to allow the sap of his Word and his Spirit to ow through us. It is to be like Moses, who refused to advance unless the presence of the Lord went with him. (See Exodus 33:15–16.) To remain in him is to seek his wisdom and enabling in all we do. The power for fruitfulness in service is not our own strength; it is in the presence of the Holy Spirit owing through us. We must remain plugged into the source of our strength and enabling. Nothing must separate us from him. If we want to be fruitful, we must remain connected to the vine. We must resist every temptation to take matters into our own hands. Our strength is found in the vine.

Jesus warns us that we can do nothing outside of abiding in him (verse 5). It is true that unbelieving doctors and counselors can alleviate pain and suffering on a physical and emotional level. Medicine and counseling can heal the hurts of a mind wounded by abuse and violence and retrain it to respond differently. We can reduce the pain of humankind in regard to poverty or suffering. All these efforts are to be applauded. When Jesus tells us that we can do nothing outside of abiding in him he is telling us that we owe everything to him. On a very basic level he is telling us that we are absolutely dependant upon him for every breath we take and every effort we make. On another level, however, he is telling us that if we want to accomplish his work in this world it must be done through abiding in him. We must learn to listen to him and his leading. We must draw upon his strength and enabling. We must surrender to the ministry of his Spirit in us. No lasting spiritual fruit can be produced through the efforts of the flesh. If we want to useful for the kingdom of God we must learn to draw all we need from the Vine.

Notice here the promise of the Lord Jesus to those who remain in him. He tells us that we can ask him anything and he will do it (verse 7). The person who remains in Christ is one who seeks the glory of Christ. The greatest desire of this individual is that the Lord Jesus be honored. This person has surrendered completely to the Lord to be an instrument of his power and enabling. It is in the context of remaining in Christ that we can ask anything of him. There are times when we separate ourselves from the Vine and ask for things outside of his will and purpose. The promise here is for those who remain in the Vine. When our heart's sincere desire is to do the will of the Lord in every area of our lives and we have surrendered our all for this purpose, we can expect that God will answer our prayers. It is the Father's will that we bear much fruit. When we ask him to grant us spiritual fruit for his glory, we can expect that he will do it.

The question you need to ask yourself is this: Are you remaining in the Lord? Do you know the power of his presence in your life? Has he been pruning you with the purpose of producing more fruit? Maybe as a Christian, you have been holding back and refusing the Lord access to certain areas of your life. The result of this is that you are becoming spiritually unproductive in your life. If you want to be spiritually healthy, you will have to allow the Lord to prune the dead wood in your life. You will have to learn to remain in him and let him fill you with his holy, enabling presence. Don't rush ahead of him. Don't resist what he wants to do in you. Yield to him. Seek him in everything you do. Don't move ahead without him. Learn the art of abiding in him.

For Consideration:

- Are there any areas of your life that you know need to be pruned? What are they?

- Has the Word of God been pruning you? In the last few days what has God been saying to you through his Word?

- How can you tell whether you are living and working in your own strength or in the strength of the Lord?

- What does it mean to remain in the Lord Jesus and his Word?

For Prayer:

- Surrender your life afresh to the Lord Jesus. Tell him that you would like him to have full control of every part of your life.

- Ask the Lord to forgive you for the times you have tried to live this life in your own strength. Ask him to teach you what it means to allow him to work and flow through you.

- Ask the Lord to teach you more of what it means to remain in him and not to run ahead of him.

40

Remain in My Love

Read John 15:9–17

Jesus had been telling his disciples that they were to remain in the vine so they could produce fruit. Apart from him, they could do nothing. Here in this passage he spoke of his love for them and called them to remain in his love.

How do we remain in the love of the Lord? Jesus answered this question in John 14:23: "If anyone loves me, he will obey my teaching. My Father will love him, and we will come to him and make our home with him." He said the same thing in John 15:10: "If you obey my commands, you will remain in my love, just as I have obeyed my Father's commands and remain in his love."

There is a very strong connection between remaining in the love of Christ and obeying his commandments. This leads us to ask the question: What is it about obedience that proves our love for the Lord? There are two points I would like to make about this.

First, obedience proves that we are in communion with Christ. You cannot obey what you do not understand or hear. Obedience proves that we have entered into a close relationship with our master and that we are hearing and listening to his voice. Disobedience, on the other hand, shows that our relationship with the Lord has been broken. It shows that we are listening to voices other than his.

Second, obedience requires sacrifice. If I am to be obedient to the Lord, it will require that I die to self and put his will before my own. This is an act of love. If you love someone, you will sacrifice your time and resources for them. When I am obedient to the Lord, I prove that I am willing to put aside my own ideas and desires and follow him. Disobedience, on the other hand, is proof that I love my possessions or my ambitions in life more than the one who saved me. The measure of my love for another is how much I am willing to deny myself or sacrifice my possessions for that individual.

Obedience to the Word of the Lord enables us to remain in the love of God. We need to understand here that the love of the Lord Jesus for us never changes. He loves the wanderer as much as he loves the faithful believer. The story of the prodigal son proves this. (See Luke 15.) While Christ's love for us will never change, our experience of that love varies. You can live in that love and delight in it on a daily basis, or you can walk away from it. You may choose to run into his loving arms and feel the warmth and security of his presence, or you may hold back and shun his love.

When Jesus tells us to remain in his love, he shows us the desire of his heart. It is his delight to love us. He wants to be in constant communion with us. It rejoices his heart to hold us close and speak to us. It breaks his heart when he sees us wander from his love.

To remain in his love is to stay in that place of communion. It is to be in a place where we can hear his voice. There in that place the Lord reveals himself to us. There in that place he pours himself on us. There we experience his power. There he teaches us about himself and his purposes. It is a place of intimacy and tremendous joy. There we feel close, secure, and loved. There we are empowered, reassured, and cleansed.

Notice in verse 11 that the reason Jesus tells us these things is so that our joy might be full. If we are to experience the joy of the Lord, it will only be in the context of remaining in his love through obedience. Those who live in disobedience cannot experience this joy. Joy only comes when we are in communion with the Savior. Sin breaks that communion. To remain in the love of the Lord is to remain in communion with him. Those who live in this place of intimate communion with their Lord will know his joy in their hearts.

Closely related to our love for God is our love for each other. His command to us here is that we love each other as he loved us. To love in this way is to follow the example of Christ who did not hesitate to die for us. Jesus goes as far as to say that the greatest expression of love for one's neighbor is that a person "lay down his life" (verse 13). The natural result of remaining in the love of the Lord is that we will find ourselves loving our neighbors as Jesus loves us.

Jesus told his disciples that though they were his servants, he considered them to be his friends (verse 15). Jesus had every right to see his disciples as servants, but he treated them as friends. The difference between a servant and a friend has to do with the communication that exists between them. It also has to do with the willingness of both parties to sacrifice themselves for each other. Jesus did not hesitate to share all that the Father had given him with his disciples. He opened himself up to his disciples as a friend with a friend. He also did not hesitate to lay down his life for his disciples in an act of loving sacrifice.

When Jesus told his disciples that he saw them as friends, he was speaking of the intimacy that existed between them. Though the Lord could so easily have seen his disciples as servants, he wanted a friendship with them instead.

Some people emphasize that believers are only servants of God. They see the relationship as that of a servant who obeys a master without question. For them God is great and holy and sometimes very distant. While they are faithful servants, these individuals often have fallen short in regard to the joy of communion with the Lord. Like Martha, they are very busy in service but miss the joy of fellowship.

Others emphasize their friendship with God. These individuals seem to enjoy intimacy with God. They know the joy of fellowship and sharing. They, however, can sometimes fall short in understanding the awesomeness and holiness of God. Somehow, we need to find a healthy balance between being a servant and being a friend of God.

Jesus called his disciples as friends to go out and bear fruit that would last (verse 16). To enable them to accomplish this task, the Lord Jesus promised that the Father would give them all they asked in his name. They had the complete authority of the Father to do the task to which they had been called. If they lacked anything, they could simply ask the Father in the name of Christ, and it would be given to them. God's storehouses would be opened and his riches placed at the disposal of his friends, so that there would be no hindrance in accomplishing their calling. God has promised that the work to which he has called us will never suffer for lack of resources.

In the midst of this discussion on bearing fruit and asking anything in the name of Christ is this simple statement of verse 17: "Love one another." At first glance, it appears to be out of place. In reality, it is the very essence of bearing fruit for the Lord. If you do not remain in the love of Christ, you will not be able to love your brother or sister as you ought. If you do not love your brother or sister, you will never be able to in uence them for the Lord.

All too often we get the cart before the horse. We place the emphasis on bearing fruit and tend to forget remaining in love. Abiding in the love of Christ is the power behind our service for the Lord. If we want to in uence people for the cause of Christ and produce fruit that will last for an eternity, then we need to spend much time before the Lord asking him to pour out his love in our hearts for our brothers and sisters. We need to spend much time before the Lord listening to him and asking for his enabling to live in complete obedience to his will. Nothing must stop us from loving the Lord with all our hearts, souls and minds. When we love him and allow him to shed his love abroad in our hearts, the results will be visible for all to see.

Do you want to be effective in service for the Lord Jesus? Remain in his love. Let his love fill your heart. Do not let disobedience break down your communion with him. It is only when we remain in the communion which love brings that we can be useful to our Master and Friend.

For Consideration:

- Have you been remaining in the love of the Lord? How has this affected your life?

- What does this passage tell you about the desire of God for you to remain in his love? What does it tell you about the relationship he wants to have with you?

- Consider the teaching of Jesus here regarding the role of servant and friend. Who is Jesus to you today?

- Why is it important to remain in the love of the Lord? Is it possible to wander from the experience of that love? What is the result?

For Prayer:

- Thank the Lord for his desire to have such intimate communion with you.

- Ask the Lord to help you draw nearer to him. Ask him to show you anything that would keep you from drawing closer to him.

- Is there anyone you have trouble loving? Ask the Lord to give you a deeper love for that person.

41

Following the Master

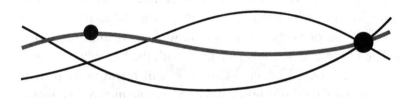

Read John 15:18–16:4

Jesus had been speaking to his disciples about remaining in his love. To remain in the love of the Lord would require that they live in obedience to his Word. As they remained in his love, they would be powerful witnesses in a lost world. Jesus reminded them, however, that the world would very likely hate them. They would be rejected for belonging to Jesus.

The life of Christ in us is like light to a creature of the night. I go back to my illustration of the bugs I found under the rock when I was a child. When struck by the light, the natural tendency of these bugs was to run for the cover of darkness. The life of Christ challenges the unbelieving world. Our purity of life confronts the immorality of the day. The Word of God, on which we base our lives, is a threat to a society where people do what is right in their own eyes. To love the Lord Jesus is to obey him and to stand up for his Word. When you and I stand up for the Word of God, we will inevitably encounter opposition.

Jesus reminded his disciples here that if they were like the world, the world would love them as its own. God had called them out of the world (verse 19). They now belonged to the Lord Jesus. As those who belonged to the Lord, they no longer chased after the things of the world, as they formerly did. Their affections were now set on the things of God. Their ambitions were no longer for the things that perish but for the things of heaven. Priorities had changed. The Lord Jesus now meant more to them than anything this world could ever offer. This change baf es the world. The world cannot understand the change that takes place in the life of the one who comes to know the salvation of Christ. The world can no longer identify with the believer.

If the world rejected Christ, it will reject us also. If it persecuted the Lord Jesus, it will persecute us too. The world will do this because it does not know the Father (verse 21). It has never experienced his love and forgiveness. It does not know the reality of his presence.

This does not excuse the world. God has revealed himself to every individual so that all are without excuse. The Lord Jesus came to earth to reveal the Father, but men rejected him. All of creation speaks of a creator to whom we owe our existence. The Bible tells us that we were created in the image and nature of God. Because we were created in his image, our whole being cries out for him. We cannot be fulfilled in our existence without God. Humankind, however, has sought to find fulfillment in the pleasures of this world.

Verses 22–24 are difficult to understand. Jesus tells us that if he had not spoken to these individuals and performed miracles in their sight, they would not be guilty of sin. This statement merits some careful consideration. God has done everything to reveal himself to humanity. If this were not so, there would be no basis for condemnation. The apostle Paul tells us in Romans 4:15: "Because the law brings wrath. And where there is no law there is no transgression."

Where there is no law, there can be no enforcement of that law. Where there is no obligation, there can be no penalty for not meeting up to that obligation. If God had not laid down his law and placed a responsibility on us to follow and honor him, then there would be no reason to punish us. We would live and die like the animals with no hope beyond the grave. God has chosen us, however, and called us to be his people. We are under an obligation to God. He has reached out to us. He has laid his life down for us on the cross. He has called us to be his children and to live with him forever. This places us under a real obligation. With great privilege comes great obligation. As those who have been called by God, we are accountable to him. We are held responsible for our sin and disobedience.

In verses 26–27 Jesus told his disciples that when the Holy Spirit came on them, they were to join the other witnesses God had left to testify of his love and to offer forgiveness. God's Word, his image in the human heart, the natural creation, the Holy Spirit, and the life and ministry of the Lord Jesus are sufficient witnesses to condemn anyone who rejects their voices. God, however, calls you and me to join this amazing team of witnesses in proclaiming the Lord Jesus as Savior and Lord. God gives us every opportunity to receive the Lord Jesus and his forgiveness. God has called us to a place of privilege and honor. He now holds us accountable to him.

Jesus reminded his disciples that this task of being his witnesses would not be easy (16:1–4). They would be publicly shamed by being cast out of the synagogue. Some of them would have to die so that the message of salvation could go out to the world.

If you know him as your Lord and Savior today, you are called to be his witness. You have been chosen by God to shine for him in a dark and sinful world. Don't be ashamed of the truth. Let that light shine brightly. You are part of

God's overall plan to reveal himself to men and women who do not know him. This may lead to opposition, but the exhortation of these passages is to stand firm as proud followers of the Master.

We are, as those who know the truth, under a tremendous obligation. God has spared no expense to reveal himself to us. May we be faithful to him.

For Consideration:

- Have you ever suffered for standing up for the Lord Jesus? Explain.

- What is it that causes you to be afraid or ashamed to stand up for the Lord today?

- How did the Lord Jesus reveal himself to you?

- What is our obligation toward God, as those who have come to know him?

- How has God been revealing himself to this world? What obligation does this put the world under?

For Prayer:

- Ask him to give you a boldness to stand for him.

- Take a moment to pray for a friend or loved one who is still resisting the truth of the Word of God.

- Ask God to show you more clearly your role as a witness to the Lord Jesus.

- Take a moment to thank the Lord for the way he has spared no expense in revealing himself to humanity.

42

The Threefold Ministry of the Holy Spirit

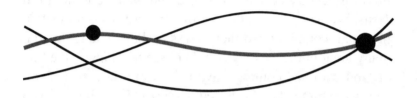

Read John 16:5–16

After Jesus had first told his disciples that he was going to leave them, Peter asked him where he was going (13:36). Later, Thomas had also asked the Lord where he was going (14:5). On this occasion, however, when Jesus repeated this same thought, no one dared to ask him where he was going. Maybe they were coming to accept what he was saying. From verse 6, however, we understand that on hearing again that Jesus was leaving them, the disciples were filled with sorrow. This was understandable, considering the fact that the disciples had left everything to follow Jesus. For three years they had given him their lives. They had grown to love and depend on him. Jesus had a profound impact on their lives. Their lives were forever changed.

Sensing their sorrow, the Lord told them that it was good that he was going away. Unless he left, the Holy Spirit could not come to them. The only way the Holy Spirit could come to them was by means of the death and resurrection of our Lord Jesus. The Spirit of God would come to live in the lives of those forgiven and cleansed by the sacrificial work of the Lord Jesus. The Holy Spirit would continue the work the Lord Jesus had begun in their lives. The Counselor would come to convict men of sin, righteousness, and judgment (verse 8). Let us examine this threefold ministry of the Holy Spirit in some detail.

First, the Holy Spirit convicts of sin. Verse 9 tells us that this is necessary because people do not believe in the Lord Jesus. We have seen in the life of our Lord Jesus how often men and women turned their backs on him. Though he did many great miracles, they could not see that he was the Son of God who had come to save them from their sins. Their eyes were blinded to their need of Christ. They did not even believe themselves to be sinners. The Holy Spirit was sent to make it possible for men and women to see their need of a Savior. He came to convict people of sin. He came to make them see that the only possible means of forgiveness for them was through the cross of the Lord Jesus.

Does the Spirit of God live in your heart? If he does, you will be convicted of sin. If you do not believe you are a sinner, you will never see your need of a Savior. As I have grown in my understanding of the work and ministry of the Holy Spirit, I have come to realize that I am a far greater sinner than I ever thought I was. There are times when I have wondered how many more sins the Spirit of God could find hidden away in the inner recesses of my life. If you are being convicted of sin, be encouraged. This is one of the clear evidences of the presence of the Holy Spirit in your life. Do you want to know if a certain work is inspired and being blessed of the Holy Spirit? Submit it to this first test. Does this work or ministry bring people to an awareness and repentance of sin? This is the first ministry of the Holy Spirit.

The second great ministry of the Holy Spirit, according to Jesus, is to convict men and women of righteousness. Verse 10 tells us why it was necessary for the Holy Spirit to exercise this ministry. The Lord Jesus was going to the Father and would no longer be with the disciples. He had taught them what it meant to live for the Father. He had instructed them in the ways of righteousness. Now that he was leaving, the disciples would need a teacher. This is why the Holy Spirit came. He came to instruct believers during the physical absence of the Lord Jesus. The Lord had already told his disciples that the Holy Spirit would bring to their remembrance the things he had taught them (14:26).

In verse 7, the Holy Spirit is called "the Counselor." A counselor is one who instructs us in the way we should go. This is the work of the Holy Spirit. When the Holy Spirit comes to live in our hearts, he brings new understanding of the Word of God. He opens our minds to the truth of the Word and the will of God. He brings to our lives a hunger for the truth. He leads us to do what is pleasing to the Lord Jesus. We find ourselves desiring to live out this truth in our lives. This is the ministry of the Holy Spirit. He comes to show us what is right. He comes to stir our hearts to seek after the will and purpose of God. He comes to be our counselor in righteousness.

Do you want to know if the Holy Spirit is living in your life? Do you hunger for the Word of God? Is the Bible coming alive to you? Do you find yourself living in obedience to the principles of God's Word? Any work that is inspired by the Holy Spirit causes men and women to live righteous and godly lives. It is the ministry of the Holy Spirit to teach us and instruct us in the ways of truth and righteousness.

The third ministry of the Holy Spirit is to convict the world of judgment. Verse 11 gives us the reason for this ministry. He convicts the world of judgment, "because the prince of this world now stands condemned."

Who is the prince of this world? This title is applied to Satan (John 12:31; 14:30; Ephesians 2:2; 6:12). John 8:44 tells us that Satan is the father of lies and deceit. Before the death of Christ, whole nations were lost in sin. Even among God's chosen people, many did not believe. Satan had also blinded them to the truth about the Lord Jesus. With the death of Christ, however, things were to change. When Christ overcame Satan on the cross, the Spirit of God began to move across the face of the earth, as never before. The message of salvation through Jesus Christ spread from nation to nation. People all over the world have come to see the truth. The deception of Satan is being revealed. Satan has been judged. The cross of Calvary has defeated him.

It is the ministry of the Holy Spirit to convince the world of the judgment of the prince of this world. Christ has overcome Satan. His power and authority have been crushed. Christ reigns supreme. Even as Satan has been judged, so his followers will too be judged. The Holy Spirit comes to bring the conviction of the lordship of Christ over Satan, the world, sin, and death.

Do you want to know if the Holy Spirit is living in your heart? Do you recognize that Jesus is Lord? Do you bow down to him who has overcome all your enemies? Does your heart over ow in praise and worship because Jesus is Lord of all? Are you living in the reality of Satan's defeat? Any work inspired by the Holy Spirit will bring conviction to the hearts of men and women that Jesus is Lord. It will inspire them to live in the victory he has brought over the prince of this world. Those who have been convicted of the judgment of Satan live in the victory that knowledge brings. Is this your experience? Why live in defeat when the enemy has already been conquered?

The threefold ministry of the Holy Spirit is to convict us of our sin, teach us what it means to live righteously, and reassure us of the absolute lordship of Christ. Does the Holy

Spirit live in your heart? If he does, you will often hear him speak to you about your sin. Do not grieve him by refusing to listen to his voice. If the Holy Spirit lives in your heart, there will be evidence of righteousness in your life. As he teaches you from the Word, your life will no longer be the same. You will be changed from within as he instructs you in the way of righteousness. If the Holy Spirit dwells within, you will be reassured in the trials of life of the absolute lordship of Christ. This will bring comfort to your soul. He will remind you that your enemy has been judged and has no ultimate power over you. You can rest in the assurance that the Lord has overcome. This is the ministry of the Holy Spirit.

There was much more that the Lord Jesus wanted to teach his disciples, but he left this to the Holy Spirit. He reminded his disciples that the Holy Spirit would speak on his behalf and bring glory to the Lord Jesus by revealing Christ and his will to them.

For Consideration:

- What evidence is there of the presence and power of the Holy Spirit in your life? Are there areas of your life where you need to see a deeper work of his Spirit? What are they?

- Can you see evidence of the presence and power of the Holy Spirit in the life of your church?

- What is the role of the Holy Spirit today according to this passage?

For Prayer:

- Thank the Lord that he has left his Holy Spirit to instruct and to guide you.

- Ask the Lord to make you more sensitive to the working of the Holy Spirit in your life.

- Ask the Holy Spirit to pour himself out on his church in conviction of sin, instruction in righteousness, and assurance of the lordship of Christ.

43

Speaking in Proverbs

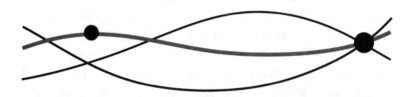

Read John 16:17–33

J esus had been telling his disciples that he was going to leave them and go to his Father. He reminded them, however, that he would not leave them as orphans. He would send the Holy Spirit to be their counselor and comforter. The disciples were confused. They did not understand what Jesus was telling them. They questioned each other about the meaning of his words. His speech was often difficult to understand.

Jesus knew that the disciples could not understand what he was saying about leaving them. He offered a further explanation: "You will weep and mourn while the world rejoices. You will grieve, but your grief will turn to joy. A woman giving birth to a child has pain because her time has come; but when her baby is born she forgets the anguish because of her joy that a child is born into the world" (verses 20–21). The explanation of Jesus to the simple statement of his going away seemed only to complicate the issue for the disciples. I would have loved to have seen the look on the faces of these men as Jesus went through this explanation. They were more confused than they had been at first. Jesus knew what he had done. In verse 25 he revealed to the disciples that he spoke figuratively. Jesus knew that his words could not be easily understood. He reminded them, however, that the day was coming when he would no longer have to speak to them in this way; instead, he would speak to them plainly.

Why did Jesus not speak plainly to his disciples at this point? Why did he feel compelled to speak to them figuratively, in parables and proverbs? According to Mark 4:33–34, this was his custom: "With many similar parables Jesus spoke the word to them, as much as they could understand. He did not say anything to them without using a parable. But when he was alone with his own disciples, he explained everything."

At one point, the disciples had asked the Lord why he had adapted this teaching style: "Why do you speak to the people in parables?" Jesus replied: "The knowledge of the secrets of the kingdom of heaven has been given to you, but not to them" (Matthew 13:10–11). Jesus knew that humankind, without the Spirit of God, would never be able to grasp the things of God. The apostle Paul spoke about this in 1 Corinthians 1:18: "For the message of the cross is foolishness to those who are perishing, but to us who are being saved it is the power of God." Spiritual matters cannot be understood by secular minds. This is why the world, under the domination of Satan, has rejected God. The natural mind cannot possibly understand the things of God: "The man without the Spirit does not accept the things that come from the Spirit of God, for they are foolishness to him, and he cannot understand them, because they are spiritually discerned" (1 Corinthians 2:14).

At this point in time, the disciples had not yet received

the Holy Spirit. Jesus had told them that when the Holy Spirit came to them, he would bring to their minds what he had told them in parables. (See John 14:26.) While the disciples had learned much under the ministry of the Lord Jesus, they would learn even more when he sent them the Holy Spirit. Jesus revealed the truth, but the Holy Spirit would bring understanding of that revealed truth.

Jesus spoke to the disciples in earthly terms because they were not yet ready to receive the deeper truths. They could understand that he was going to leave them, but they could not understand the implications of his leaving. They knew what it meant for Jesus to die, but they could not understand the reason behind his death. Like little children, they were not ready for deeper explanations. He used simple illustrations of everyday earthly things so they could understand.

In verse 20 Jesus told his disciples that they would weep and mourn while the rest of the world rejoiced. Jesus was referring to his death in this verse. The death of the Lord Jesus would be a source of great joy for the Jewish leaders. They saw Jesus as a threat. They did not want him in their presence. The disciples, on the other hand, would feel great pain at the death of their Lord. They would lose a dear friend and master. Jesus reminded them, however, that their mourning would be turned to joy. The Lord Jesus would be raised from the dead. Death would have no final victory over him. Because he would conquer death, his followers would have the hope of victory over death. Because he would conquer death, his followers would be assured that sin which had brought death to mankind was also conquered. This would be a reason for great rejoicing. Like a mother who gives birth to a young child, there is great pain in the birthing process, but when the child is born the pain turns to great rejoicing. The disciples would groan under the weight of the death of Christ, but their pain would quickly turn to joy that no one would ever be able to take away. Their Lord would conquer death.

In verses 25–28 the Lord told his disciples plainly that he was going to his Father. This is what he meant when he told them that in a while they would no longer see him. Notice the result of Jesus' return to the Father and his victory over sin and death: "In that day you will ask in my name, I am not saying that I will ask the Father on your behalf" (verse 26). Christ's death would restore fellowship between the Father and his children—we now have direct access to God. We can approach the Father directly because of what the Lord Jesus has done. What a joy it is to know that we can be accepted by the Father because of the work of his Son on our behalf.

These comments seemed to clear up some confusion for the disciples. They were reassured in their faith concerning the Lord Jesus and the fact that he came from God. They stated that Jesus did not need anyone to ask him anything because he already knew their needs before they asked (verse 30). They saw him as an all-knowing God. Did they make this statement because Jesus had understood their confusion (verse 18)? They had not told him about their confusion, and yet he knew that they did not understand. He knew their hearts and minds. He knew what troubled them even before they had told him about it. This confirmed his deity to them.

The disciples told Jesus that they believed that he was from God (verse 30). As admirable as this statement was, it would be put to the test. This conviction that Jesus was the Son of God would cause the disciples many problems. In just a short while, the Jews would come and arrest Jesus and the disciples would leave him. This would be only the beginning of their troubles. They would have to endure much for the sake of the Lord Jesus and their belief that he was the Son of God. Jesus reassured them, however, that they were not to fear, for they were his and he had overcome the world (verse 33).

What a difference it would make in the lives of these disciples when the Holy Spirit would come to rest on each of them at Pentecost (Acts 2:3). He would bring to them an understanding of truth that they had never experienced before. You cannot read the letters of the apostles without being struck by their absolute assurance of the truth that Jesus had taught them. These same disciples stood before the Lord that day needing to be spoon-fed because they could not understand the full implication of the truth Jesus taught them. They would later preach that same truth with such conviction and depth of understanding that it would baf e the minds of those who heard them. These disciples would be willing to die for what the Lord had taught them.

For Consideration:

• Look back to the days before you came to know the Lord Jesus as your Savior and knew the indwelling of his Holy Spirit. What did you understand about the Word of God? What difference has the Holy Spirit made in your understanding of spiritual things?

• What does this passage teach you about the ministry of the Holy Spirit in the lives of the disciples? How does this apply to you today?

For Prayer:

• Thank the Lord for the gift of his Holy Spirit to help you understand his Word and his will.

• Thank him that he understands your needs even before you share them with him.

- Ask him to give you an increasing love for his Word. Ask him to help you to stand firmly on it.

- Ask the Lord to help you to understand and experience to an even greater extent the counseling and teaching ministry of the Holy Spirit in your life.

44

Father, Glorify Your Son

Read John 17:1–5

The time for Jesus to die was rapidly approaching. In just a few short hours, he would be arrested and brought to trial. He knew his time was short. How would you spend your last hours of life? Jesus spent the time with his Father in prayer. In the next few meditations we will examine the prayer of Jesus. In this first section of Jesus' prayer, he prayed for himself.

As Jesus began to pray, he lifted his eyes to heaven. Where is God? Is he not everywhere present? Why did Jesus lift his eyes toward heaven? This appears to be a Jewish custom. In Ezekiel 1:25–28 the prophet Ezekiel looked upward to see the glory of the One seated on the throne. In Psalm 121:1–2 the Psalmist tells us that he would lift his eyes to the hills toward the Lord to seek his help. God was seen as coming down to Mount Sinai in the days of Moses (Exodus 19:11). When the veil of the temple was ripped in two, it was ripped from the top to the bottom, that is, from

God to man (Matthew 27:51). In the Jewish mind, heaven was above and that was where God lived. This is not to say that God can be confined to one place. We know that he is everywhere present.

Jesus asked the Father to glorify the Son (verse 1). What does it mean to glorify someone? To glorify an individual is to bring honor to that individual or to cause that person's worth to become evident. Notice the reason Jesus wanted to be glorified. He wanted to be glorified so that he might bring glory to the Father. Can we pray this prayer of Jesus today? My first reaction is that this is a prayer that only our Lord Jesus could have prayed. As believers, we are uncomfortable with the idea of receiving glory.

When Jesus prayed that the Father would glorify him, what was he asking? Was he not asking that the purposes and power of the Father be revealed in his life? When the power of God is demonstrated in our lives, people will take notice. When the Spirit of God works powerfully in our lives, we will be a blessing to those around us. The truth is that when the Lord Jesus glorifies himself in us, we share in that glory. We become the instrument in which that glory shines. We ought never to be ashamed of being everything the Lord wants us to be. Should we fear to pray that the Father would make his glory evident in our lives? Should we fear to pray that our lives would be filled with the glory of God? The apostle Paul ran the Christian race as one seeking the prize (Philippians 3:14). He wanted to receive the applause at the end of the race. He wanted to hear the Father tell him, "Well done". If we persevere to the end, we will be honored by the Father. What a joy it will be to know that the Father is pleased with us. What a joy it will be to receive our rewards. What satisfaction it will bring to our souls to know that our lives counted for the glory of God.

Having said this, we need to be careful to follow the example of our Lord Jesus. Why did he want to be glorified?

He wanted to be glorified for the sake of the Father. If we do not run to win, the Father will not receive the glory. If our lives do not stand out in the crowd as different, then the Father does not receive the praise. If our gifts are not being used to the maximum, then we do not honor God as we ought. God is honored in us when we shine with his glory in the darkness of this sinful world. The reason we run the race to win is not because of the glory we will receive ourselves, but because of the glory it will bring to our heavenly Father. Our value is made evident when our lives shine with the glory of God. The purpose for which we were created is to glorify God. It is in glorifying us (making evident our value as his servants) that God himself is glorified in the world.

Jesus wanted the glory of the Father to be evident in his life. He strove to be everything he could be for the Father so that through his life the Father would be glorified. Our passage tells us that Jesus would bring glory to the Father by giving eternal life to those whom the Father had given him. These individuals in turn would honor God and praise him for eternity. The task of the Lord Jesus was to present God to those whom the Father had given him and to open the door for them to be glorified by the Father.

Jesus then prayed that he would receive the glory that he had with the Father before the world began (verse 5). What does this request tell us about Jesus? It tells us that he was with God before the world began. It tells us that he shared the glory of God. It reminds us of the great cost of our redemption. Jesus, the Son of God, was with God before the world began, sharing in the glory of the Father. He left the glory of heaven to be crucified by mankind. For thirty years he put that glory aside. Now, however, Jesus was going to return to the Father and share again in the glory he once knew.

The Father would lift up his Son and give him a name that was greater than any other name. The Lord Jesus would be exalted. He had, by his death and resurrection, accomplished the greatest work of all time, the redemption of mankind from the hands of Satan. From that point forth, as humanity looked at the glorified Jesus Christ, they would be reminded of the great redemptive plan of God. For eternity they would exalt and praise the Father for the work of the Son.

The honor the Lord Jesus received brought glory to his Father. God was glorified because of Jesus' faithfulness to the end. His glorious life pointed people to the Father. It was his greatest desire that the glory of his Father be demonstrated in his life. He received glory so that the Father, in return, would be glorified.

What about us? Will we allow the power and enabling of the Spirit of God to change us and make us into new and glorious creatures? Will we be willing to step out in that glory and make our lives count by drawing men and women to the Father?

Let me illustrate this point by means of a simple illustration. Our lives are like a circular tube that finds its source in God, is stretched out into the world, and then returns to God. As the life of God circulates in the tube, the tube itself shines with the glory of that life. The thing about the tube however, is that it is not a container. It does not keep the glory for itself. The glory ows through the tube but always returns to the source. This is what God is calling us to be. We are the instruments through which his glory will be demonstrated to the world. We share in his glory as he ows through us, but we keep none of it for ourselves. We pray, therefore, that God would glorify us so that we might share in that glory and bring honor to his name.

For Consideration:

• To what extent is the glory of the Father evident in your life? How is it evident in you?

- What obstacles stand between you and the glory of the Father being revealed in you?

- Why is it so hard for us to accept the fact that God wants to glorify us so that we can in turn glorify him?

- Is it possible to live in humility and experience the glory of God flowing through us? How do we keep humble as God works in us and through us?

For Prayer:

- Pray that the glory of the Father will be revealed in you so that the Father will be glorified through you.

- Ask the Lord to forgive you for not revealing that glory of the Father as you should.

- Take a moment to pray that your local church would experience this glory of the Father.

- Ask God to keep you humble as you demonstrate the glory of the Father in the world.

45

Jesus' Prayer for His Disciples

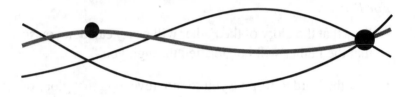

Read John 17:6–19

We will look now at the second part of Jesus' prayer to the Father. The focus of Jesus in this second section of his prayer was the eleven disciples who had faithfully served him for the last three years. Judas was not included with the other disciples in this prayer because verse 12 tells us that he was lost and doomed for destruction. For our purposes we will divide Jesus' prayer into two parts: Who were these disciples? and What did Jesus pray for his disciples?

Who Were These Disciples?

Our Lord has many things to tell us here about his disciples. First, he tells us that they had been given to Jesus by the Father (verse 6). Jesus was speaking here about the eleven faithful disciples in particular. These men had been chosen, even before they were born, for the ministry to which the Father had called them. They were born for a purpose. These men had a very definite sense of calling from God. They were in the ministry because they had received a commission from him. The prophet Jeremiah also had this experience. The Lord told him that even before he was born, he had been called to be a prophet to the nations (Jeremiah 1:5).

Second, the disciples had obeyed the Word (verse 6). God had chosen them for a particular ministry, but that was not enough. There was another qualification necessary here. These men had obeyed the Word of God. Not only were they called, they were also obedient. Both characteristics are required in a servant of God. There is nothing that will disqualify us from service more than disobedience.

Third, his disciples knew with certainty who Jesus was (verses 7–8). While they may have had some doubts in the beginning, this could not be said about them now. For the most part, these men felt they were ready to stand up and die for the name of the Lord Jesus. They believed him to be the Son of God. They believed his Word to be true.

Fourth, they glorified the Lord Jesus (verse 10). These disciples had a new goal in life. They wanted, more than anything else, to bring glory to the name of the Lord Jesus. By their lives and words, they would spread the message of the lordship of Jesus Christ over sin, Satan, and the grave. These men would live and die for the glory of their Lord. They were not in the ministry for themselves. They were in it to glorify the Lord Jesus.

Fifth, because of their stand, they were hated by the world (verse 14). They had been rescued from sin and brought into a new relationship with the Lord Jesus. Their allegiance was no longer to the world but to their new master. Their ambitions and their goals in life were radically transformed by this new power working in them. The world could not identify with them. Because they would often stand in opposition to the world, they would be hated by the world.

Finally, they had been sent into the world (verse 18). Though foreigners to the world, they were called to go into it with the message of the gospel of the Lord Jesus. They were chosen to be ambassadors for the Lord Jesus to a world in need. These were individuals who had a burden for the lost. They would do much for the church of Christ, but they were not sent to the church only. They were also sent to reach those who had never heard the message of the gospel.

What Did Jesus Pray for His Disciples?

Let's consider the second part of Jesus' prayer for his disciples. Jesus brought his requests for his disciples to his heavenly Father. First, Jesus prayed that his Father would protect them (verses 11–12). As we have already mentioned, these disciples were no longer part of the world. The world hated them. They would have to face much opposition from the world. Jesus asked his Father to place his protective hand on his disciples so that they could accomplish the tasks to which he had called them. It was the will of the Lord Jesus that none of them be lost. It was his desire that these men be kept by the power of God until they had fulfilled their heavenly mandate on earth.

Though these men were not part of the world, the world was still a real temptation. Jesus' prayer was also that these disciples would be protected or kept from the in uence of the world. This is a very real temptation for every servant of God. Just because we are disciples of the Lord does not mean that we no longer feel the pull of the world. Jesus prayed that his disciples would be victorious over the world and its attractions.

Second, Jesus prayed that they would be one, even as he and the Father were one (verse 11). It seems to me that this "oneness" is twofold. They were to be one with the Father and Christ, even as the Father and Christ were one in nature and purpose. Nothing was to separate the disciples from their relationship with the Father and his Son.

This "oneness" was also to be expressed in their relationship with each other. In John 13:35 Jesus told his disciples: "By this all men will know that you are my disciples, if you love one another." There is a close connection between the unity of the body of Christ and its effectiveness in the work of ministry. When there is oneness in the body, there is also victory in service. Where disunity reigns, we can only expect failure. Jesus prayed that these disciples might be one with him and each other so that nothing would hinder their ministry.

Third, Jesus prayed that they would have a full measure of joy (verse 13). The Christian life is a joyous life. In Christ there is fullness of joy. It was the desire of the Lord Jesus that his disciples experience that fullness. They would be hated by the world. The world would think that they were doing God a service by killing them. Some of them would know real pain in their lives. In the midst of all this agony, however, the joy of the Lord would over ow in their hearts.

All too often, we lose the joy of the Lord in our ministry and service. It was the desire of the Lord Jesus that his joy fill the hearts of his disciples and carry them through the difficulties of ministry and service for him. Someone once described "burnout" as losing all the "fun" in ministry. While ministry may not always be "fun," this description of burnout is truer than we might want to admit. Burnout is when we have lost the thrill and joy of service. We no longer get up in the morning with joy in our hearts for the opportunities to serve the Lord. Jesus' prayer was that his hard working servants experience a full measure of joy. Notice here that Jesus prayed for "a full measure" of joy. Do you have joy in service as a servant of God? I believe that Jesus is interceding for you right now. He is pleading with the Father to give you joy in his service.

Fourth, Jesus prayed that his disciples would be protected from the evil one (verse 15). Jesus knew that these disciples would be targets for the enemy's arrows. It was these men who would take positions on the front line, as the army of God marched into the world with the message of salvation. Satan knew that if he could destroy these leaders, then he would also wreck havoc in the camp. These disciples, as well as godly Christian leaders in our day, would be the particular focus of Satan's attack. Jesus had already prayed that the Father would shield them from the world that hated them. Then he prayed for their protection against the spiritual enemy that would assault them.

Finally, Jesus prayed that they would be sanctified by the truth (verses 17–19). To be sanctified is to be consecrated to God or to be set apart for him. It is to be drawn to God and to take on his characteristics. These disciples would be sanctified by means of the Word of God. The Word that Jesus had given them had the power to transform lives. This Word had the power to reveal sin and correct behavior. This Word could draw them closer to God. Jesus' prayer for his disciples is that they would be men of the Word. He prayed that they would become men who were committed to the study and observation of his revealed Word.

Jesus' prayer for his disciples is a real challenge for us as believers. It teaches us how we can more effectively pray for God's servants today. It teaches us that the battle is truly a spiritual one. It cannot be won without prayer. May we be willing to wage that battle for righteousness, truth, and the salvation of souls today.

For Consideration:

• Take a moment to review how Jesus prayed for his disciple. What does this reveal to you about the nature of the battle today?

- What does this passage teach us about how to pray for our Christian leaders?

- According to this passage, what are the temptations we will have to face as Christian leaders?

- What are some of the obstacles to joy in service for Christ?

For Prayer:

- Take a moment to pray for your pastor or Christian leaders. Pray for them the things that Jesus prayed for his disciples.

- Ask the Lord to bring unity to his body.

- Thank the Lord that he promised to protect you and keep you.

- Ask the Lord to give you fullness of joy in service for him.

46

Jesus Prays for Us

Read John 17:20–26

J esus had prayed for himself and his disciples. He then centered his attention on those who would believe in him because of the ministry of his disciples. Who are these people? They are all those, down through the years, who have accepted the Lord Jesus as their Lord and Savior. They are people like you and me, who believe in the Lord Jesus Christ because of his Word passed on to us through his disciples. There are three main requests that Jesus made to his Father for us in this prayer. These requests show us his heart's desire for us.

Number one on the Lord's prayer list for us is that we might "be one" (verse 21). This may seem to be a strange request to place first on the list, but if we examine it in detail, we will see how important this request really is. Note the reason why the Lord Jesus brings this request to the Father. Verse 23 tells us that it would be by this means that the world would know that the Father sent the Son and that he loved his own, even as the Father loved him. This merits careful consideration.

Have you ever thought of your relationship with your brother or sister in Christ as a proof to the world that the Father sent the Son to die on the cross of Calvary for sinners? This seems to be what the Lord was saying here. When you love your brothers and sisters with the love of the Lord, you prove that the love of Christ is in you. The only explanation for the love of God demonstrated between believers is the fact that God lives in them. The only way that this love of God can dwell in the heart of a believer is that the obstacle of sin has been removed through the work of the Lord Jesus on the cross. By loving your brothers and sisters with Christ's love, you are demonstrating to them that you have had victory over sin and self through Christ who died on the cross to set you free.

When you do not live in harmony with your brothers and sisters in the Lord, you bring dishonor on the name of our God. Have you ever had the experience of taking your children to visit someone you did not know very well? Maybe you felt somewhat uncomfortable as you arrived at the house. Before entering their home, you shared some last minute words with your children. You encouraged them to be well-behaved and not to argue among themselves. Why was it important for you that your children get along? It was important because their behavior re ected on you as parents. If you have ever left someone's home after having settled several fights among your young children, you probably felt embarrassed and upset. In the same way, our behavior as children of God re ects on God. Our behavior can cause his name to be blasphemed by those who do not know him. Jesus prayed, therefore, for the unity of the body of Christ, so that the world would know that God's love is being perfected in us.

This unity that Jesus prayed for was not only a unity

between brothers and sisters but also a unity with the Father. What Jesus was praying here was that we would be united with him in such a way that his love would ow through us to our brothers and sisters. When people see the love of God demonstrated in our lives, they are in reality seeing the work Christ is doing in us. Though they may not always be aware of it, they are seeing proof that Jesus does live in the hearts of those who accept him. Maybe you have met individuals who have powerfully re ected Christ in their lives. There is something very wonderful in the lives of these individuals. They show in a very practical way the joy, satisfaction, and power that come from being in a personal relationship with Christ.

The second request of the Lord Jesus was that those who believed in him would dwell with him and behold his glory (verse 24). It was not the will of the Lord Jesus that any of us be lost on the way. He prayed that all who would believe in him would live with him forever.

There are many temptations in the lives of believers. Often we take the wrong path when the enemy succeeds in drawing us away from the Lord. Jesus knew that it would not be easy to live for him. What a comfort it is to know, however, that he stands behind us in prayer. He pleads with the Father for us in our weakness. He petitions the Father when we are being lured away from the path of truth. It is not his will that any be lost. He wants every one of his sheep to dwell forever with him in heaven and behold him in his glory. His present ministry is one of intercession for us. The apostle Paul reminds us of this in Romans 8:34: "Who is he that condemns? Christ Jesus, who died—more than that, who was raised to life—is at the right hand of God and is also interceding for us."

Christ did not save you and leave you to fend for yourself. It is still his great concern that you grow in grace and knowledge. He knows your temptations and pain. He continues to petition the Father on your behalf for strength and enabling. He wants you to dwell with him forever. He does not want anything to keep you from him. His prayers will lead you safely home.

This third petition was not so much a request as it was a promise. Jesus committed himself to continuing to reveal the Father to us in order that the love the Father had for Jesus would be in us (verse 26). In other words, Christ promised to reveal God the Father to us in such a way that we would know his love in a very real manner. Notice also that he promised that he himself would be in us.

The prayer of Jesus for us was that we would be so united in our love for one another that the world would know that Jesus is truly among us. He also prayed that we would be kept through the trials of this life and dwell in his glorious presence forever. Finally he made a commitment to us that he would continue to work in us, revealing his Father to us. What a wonderful encouragement it is to know that Christ is still working in us. What a challenge it is, however, to let him accomplish his work in us.

For Consideration:

- Is there anyone you have trouble loving? What separates you from this person? How does this affect your witness for the Lord Jesus?

- What encouragement do you take from the fact that the Lord Jesus is praying for you today?

- Is the character and person of the Father becoming more real to you? Do you know and love him more today that ever before?

- What evidence is there that the Lord Jesus is continuing to work in you?

For Prayer:

- Ask God to heal the broken relationships in your life.

- Thank him for his desire to see you persevere in your relationship with him. Thank the Lord for his prayer for you in this regard.

- Ask the Lord to reveal the Father to you in an even greater measure.

47

Put Your Sword Away

Read John 18:1–11

His prayer finished, Jesus took his disciples to an olive grove on the other side of the Kidron Valley. Judas was not with Jesus and his disciples at this time. Judas had left them the day Jesus had washed their feet. Now he was seeking a means to betray Jesus. Though Judas was not with the disciples on this occasion, he knew where they were, for they had often gone to this olive grove. It was obviously a place of retreat for them.

On this occasion, the peaceful calm of the olive grove was broken when Judas arrived, leading a detachment of soldiers, officials, and Pharisees. The soldiers had brought weapons, lanterns, and torches. Jesus asked them whom they sought. "Jesus of Nazareth," they responded (verse 5). "I am he," said Jesus (verse 6). Those three simple words reverberated through the olive garden. The crowd of trained soldiers and officials drew back at the sound of his voice and fell to the ground (verse 6).

Why did these men fall to the ground? One explanation might be that they were surprised to find Jesus; however, this would not fit the context. They had come fully expecting to find the Lord Jesus in the olive grove, so they would not have been surprised to find him there. It is true that Jesus did not make any effort to hide himself from them. He approached them and told them who he was. Admittedly, this would have taken them by surprise. The natural response of the hunted is to hide, not to make himself known to the enemy. Though they were, no doubt, surprised by his approach, this would not necessarily have caused them to draw back and fall to the ground. Among this group were trained soldiers who were accustomed to facing the enemy.

How else can we explain the fact that this mob fell to the ground at the sound of those three words: "I am he"? Is it possible that what took place that day was of a supernatural nature? This moment was a turning point in history. This was the climax of the great battle between God and Satan. Jesus was offering himself to become the sacrificial lamb for our sins. These men standing before the Lord Jesus were going to perform the world's most hideous crime. They were going to kill the Savior of the world.

Before them stood the Son of God. It was by his breath that the world came into being (John 1:1–3). It was by that same breath that the sick were made well. When he spoke, nature itself listened and the worst of storms were calmed (Mark 4:39). At the sound of his voice, the dead were given back their life (John 11:43). When Jesus spoke that day, there was power in his words. The men present felt that power. At the sound of his voice, they were knocked to the ground. This was no ordinary man they were dealing with. He showed them that day that he could have destroyed them with a simple word, because he was God.

What a scene it was. The angry mob lay helpless on the ground in a tangled pile of human bodies. They were so stunned at what had happened that Jesus had to ask the question again. "Who is it you want?" (verse 7). There can be no doubt as to who was in control of the situation that day. The Lord Jesus himself was orchestrating the events of this encounter. As the mob untangled themselves from one another and got back on their feet, they told Jesus that they had come looking for him.

It is important to note the response of Peter to what was happening. Peter somehow did not see the hand of God in this situation. He decided he needed to help Jesus. Drawing his sword, he cut off the ear of one of the men present. It is quite likely that he would have fought to the death to defend his Lord. What Peter did not realize, however, was that the Lord did not need him to defend him. "Put your sword away," said Jesus. "Shall I not drink the cup the Father has given me?" (verse 11).

Have you ever found yourself in Peter's shoes? All around everything seems to be falling apart. The enemy is bearing down on you. You are losing your grip. Things are not turning out as you had hoped, so you take charge of matters yourself. You draw your sword and start doing battle. Maybe your motives are like Peter's. You sincerely want to help the Lord. With your drawn sword in hand, you are taking care of things the best way you know how, fighting with all the strength you can muster. Maybe you need to listen to what the Lord told Peter: "Put your sword away." Jesus was saying something like this to Peter, "This battle is not for you. It is my battle; let me handle it. Put your sword away."

Peter had not really understood what had taken place when the Lord uttered those three powerful words: "I am he." Peter had not understood that the Lord did not need his futile human efforts. The words "I am he" are powerful words. What Jesus meant by these three words was, "I am the Messiah you look for. I am the Son of God. I am your all-powerful and loving Creator. I am your Savior. I am the one you have been looking for."

This situation was in the hands of the Master of the universe. There was nothing Peter could do to make things better. His burst of human emotion had only made matters worse. He had cut off the ear of the high priest's servant. A relative of this man would later recognize Peter (verse 26). Peter would eventually deny ever having been with Jesus.

It seems to me that the great lesson of these verses is one of trust in the Lord Jesus. When faced with opposition, we all have a tendency to draw our swords and take matters into our own hands. Don't get me wrong. I am not saying that we are to sit idly by and do nothing. Peter's action, however, was totally self-motivated. He had not sought the will of the Lord in this matter. He responded out of pure human reason and emotion in his own strength. We serve a sovereign God. He is in absolute control. He chooses to use us in his way and in his time. We are his instruments. There is, however, a difference between stepping out in his authority when he calls us and drawing our swords as Peter did.

Peter fought against the purpose of God that day. He fought against the crucifixion of Jesus. This crucifixion was the reason Jesus had come to earth. It was for the salvation of our souls that he was to die. Peter stood with sword in hand, fighting so that Jesus would not have to die. He failed to see the purpose of God in what was happening that day. God's purposes are often disguised in tragedy or struggle.

May the Lord cause each of us to examine our own lives in the light of Peter's response to the arrest of Jesus. Maybe some of us need to put our swords away. Peter failed to see that the situation was already in good hands. By stepping out in his own strength, Peter was only getting in the way. Could it be that the Lord is calling us to step aside and let him do his work?

For Consideration:

- Are there situations in your life that seem to be out of control? What are they?

- Where is Jesus in these situations? Is he Lord of this situation?

- Could it be that by seeking to take control of your situation, you are in reality getting in the way?

For Prayer:

- Thank the Lord that his is in control of this universe and everything that happens.

- Commit yourself afresh to him and his loving care. Surrender your problems to him right now.

- Ask him to forgive you for getting in the way, by trying to solve your difficulties on your own.

- Thank him that he does work out all things for your good.

48

Peter's Denial

Read John 18:12–27

The mob had come to the olive grove with weapons to arrest Jesus. With them had come a detachment of soldiers and officials. They had been expecting trouble, but apart from Peter's outburst of emotion, there was no opposition. Jesus was arrested and brought to Annas, the father-in-law of Caiaphas, the high priest.

Why did the Jews bring Jesus to Annas and not to Caiaphas, the high priest? Luke 3:2 may shed some light on this matter: "During the high priesthood of Annas and Caiaphas, the word of God came to John son of Zechariah in the desert." In this verse we see that both men were high priests at this time. It may be that this reflected something of the times in which the Jews were living. Caiaphas may have been the priest recognized by the Roman government, whereas, Annas was recognized by the Jews. At any rate, we have two high priests in Jerusalem at this time. It is only in this context that we can understand this chapter.

The soldiers took Jesus to Annas (verse 13). As Jesus was being led to Annas, two of his disciples followed at a distance to see what would happen to their Lord. One of those disciples was Peter. The second disciple remains unnamed. It may be that this disciple was John, the author of this Gospel. The soldiers took Jesus into the high priest's courtyard. This meant that the two disciples would not have been able to see what was happening with Jesus. The unnamed disciple, because he knew the high priest, was granted permission to enter the courtyard. Peter, however, had to remain outside.

Possibly because of his influence, the "unnamed disciple" was able to speak to the girl on duty at the door, and she let Peter inside. When the girl saw Peter, however, she recognized him as one of Jesus' disciples. Peter flatly denied this and went into the courtyard (verse 17). He joined a group standing around a fire and listened to the proceedings.

As Peter stood by the fire, he heard the high priest question the Lord Jesus. They questioned him about his teachings and his disciples. No doubt, Peter's ears perked up when they began asking questions about Jesus' disciples. Jesus did not cooperate with the high priest. He told Annas to question those who had heard him teach. Jesus had no secret doctrines. He had openly preached and taught in the temple. Many others had heard him preach. There was no need to question him on this matter. What he said to the high priest was interpreted as being disrespectful. An official nearby struck Jesus in the face. This action was illegal, and Jesus challenged the official who struck him (verse 23).

After Annas was satisfied that he had obtained all he could out of Jesus, he sent him to his son-in-law, Caiaphas. Annas may not have had the authority to convict Jesus of any crime worthy of death. John does not describe for us what transpired when Jesus stood before Caiaphas.

What is important for us to note here is what is taking place with Peter while these proceedings with Jesus were unfolding. In a sense, there were two trials taking place simultaneously. While the Lord was being tried, Peter was having to face his own personal trial. As Peter stood around the fire warming himself, one of the other individuals present accused him of being one of Jesus' disciples. For the second time Peter denied his association with Christ.

Among those who stood around the fire was a relative of the man whose ear Peter had cut off in the olive grove. This individual had been with the mob when they had arrested Jesus. He recognized Peter as being one of Jesus' disciples. Again, Peter was asked about his association with the Lord. For the third time he denied having anything to do with Jesus. It was then that the rooster crowed (verse 27).

To understand this more fully, we need to re-examine John 13. It was here that Jesus washed the disciple's feet. During that evening meal, Jesus told the disciples that Judas would betray him, though admittedly they did not completely understand what he was saying (13:18–30). He also reminded them that he was going to die. The strongest opposition to this statement came from the lips of Peter. That night Peter boldly proclaimed that he was willing to lay down his life for his Lord (13:37). Jesus prophesied, however, that Peter would deny him three times before the rooster crowed.

When the mob had come to arrest Jesus, Peter alone took a stand. He drew his sword and stood his ground in defense of his Lord. He would have laid his life down had Jesus not stopped him and told him to put his sword away. While Peter stood his ground before a detachment of armed soldiers, he failed miserably in front of the servant girl who kept the door. Why did Peter deny Christ before the servant girl when he seemed so bold on other occasions? We can only speculate here as to a possible answer. Was it because his faith had taken a beating? The Lord Jesus was in the hands of the enemy, and it seemed that the enemy was going to have him killed. Peter's faith was being put to the test.

Perhaps Peter failed because his support structure had come out from beneath him. He felt he could no longer lean on his master as he had done in the past. Jesus had been taken away from him. His fellow disciples had fled. Did he feel helpless and alone? While we will never really have the answers to these questions, there are some important lessons for us to learn from this story of Peter.

First, we don't really know how we would respond if our support structures were torn from beneath us. It is easy to feel confident when things are going well and when friends surround us. How would we respond, however, if like Peter, all we depended on was removed? Would we too begin to crumble? We dare not place our confidence in ourselves.

Second, this story reminds us that we are all sinners in desperate need of the Savior's constant enabling. None of us can claim invincibility. Peter was the most outstanding of all the disciples. He was the one who was willing to stand up against a whole detachment of soldiers to defend his Lord. It was Peter, however, who fell first. The strong can go down as quickly as the weak.

Finally, it is important that we realize that the chain of our commitment to God is only as strong as its weakest link. Like Peter, you may come across to others as being a very strong and devoted Christian. In your life, however, you know that there is a weak link. When Satan begins to tug on the chain of your commitment to God, it does not matter how strong all the other links are. Your chain will break at the point of its weakest link. For David and Solomon the weak link was the women in their lives. For Judas it was the love of money. What is the weak link in your life?

I could have been standing around that fire; I could have been looking into the eyes of that servant girl; I could have fallen just as easily as Peter. I cannot claim to be better or stronger than the apostle Peter. My chain also has its weak links. I am constantly in need of the enabling presence of the Spirit of God in my life. If I overcome, it will only be by God's strength. I dare not trust my own. I need his enabling every moment of every day. Without him I would surely fall. The man who so boldly drew his sword to defend his Lord in our last meditation discovered that his human strength and wisdom were not sufficient. This was a powerful lesson that Peter would not soon forget. May we, like Peter, learn the weakness of our own flesh. May that awareness cause us to depend more fully upon the strength and wisdom that our Lord so delights to give all who will seek him.

For Consideration:

- Have you ever found yourself in a situation where you too were afraid to stand up for the Lord? What was it that kept you from standing up for him?

- What kind of support structure do you have? What would happen if, like Peter, your support structure was taken away from you?

- What are some of the "weak links" in your chain of commitment to Jesus?

For Prayer:

- Ask the Lord to forgive you for thinking that you can live this Christian life in your own strength.

- Ask the Lord to reveal your "weak links." Ask him to protect you and strengthen you in these areas of your life.

49

Pilate and the Crucifixion of Christ

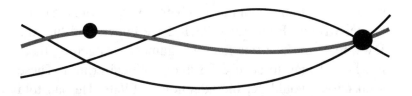

Read John 18:28–19:22

eter had denied the Lord. The other disciples had fled. Annas and Caiaphas, the high priests, had questioned Jesus. He was then led to Pilate, the Roman governor. From verse 31 we learn that the Jews did not have the right to execute a person and, therefore, needed the Roman government to do this for them.

There is an interesting paradox in this passage. The Bible tells us that because the Passover was near, the Jews refused to enter the governor's palace. If they entered a Gentile home before the Passover, they would be required by their law to undergo seven days of purification. Though they would not enter the palace for fear of defilement, they were guilty of an even greater defilement—they were about to participate in the murder of the Son of God.

Because they would not enter his palace, Pilate was obligated to come out to meet them. He questioned them about Jesus: "What charges are you bringing against this man?" (verse 29). Their response was vague: "'If he were not a criminal,' they replied, 'we would not have handed him over to you'" (verse 30). What was Pilate to do with such a statement? The Jews had no accusation here. Had they expected Pilate to approve the death penalty without any examination of the case? Had they expected that Pilate would agree to the sentence simply to please them? While it is true that Pilate would eventually bend to their wishes, he refused to do so at this point. "Take him yourselves and judge him by your own law," was his response.

To get a clearer picture of this entire scene, we will glean some information about the trial before Pilate from the other gospel writers. From Luke 23:1–2 we understand that the Jews, realizing that this line of argument was getting them nowhere, began to accuse Jesus of political crimes. These accusations would get the attention of Pilate. He had told them to judge Jesus according to their own law. Obviously, he had suspected that their accusations were of a religious nature. When they accused Jesus of claiming to be king of the Jews, however, this was a matter Pilate could not ignore. He brought Jesus into the palace for further questioning. "Are you the king of the Jews?" Pilate asked (verse 33). Jesus told Pilate that though he was king, his kingdom was not of this world. His kingdom was a heavenly kingdom. He reminded Pilate that he did not come for political reasons but rather to proclaim the truth. His kingdom consisted of those who believed the truth he taught. On hearing this, Pilate understood that Jesus posed no political threat to the Roman occupation of Israel. This problem was, as he suspected, of a religious nature. He found no basis for an accusation against Jesus. He went out to the Jews to inform them of his decision: "I find no basis for a charge against him," he concluded (verse 38).

Pilate knew that the Jews would not be content with his judgment. It was his custom to release a criminal at the time of the Passover. In an attempt to please the Jews and finally solve this problem of what to do with Jesus, Pilate decided that he would give the Jews a choice. He chose a man by the name of Barabbas to stand beside Jesus in front of the people. Barabbas was a known revolutionary. He had been in prison for insurrection and murder (Luke 23:19). This was a very shrewd political move on the part of Pilate. He knew that the crowd would not be happy with his refusal to condemn Jesus. How could he keep the people happy and not condemn Jesus whom he considered innocent? By bringing a known murderer onto the stage with Jesus, Pilate threw the decision back at the people. There is no doubt in my mind that Pilate took this action to set Jesus free and save himself from having to make an unpopular decision. The whole situation backfired on Pilate. The people called for the release of Barabbas. For us who love the Lord, this decision is hard to understand. The Jews chose to release a known murderer rather than the Lord Jesus who had healed their sick and offered them eternal life.

Because his attempt to release the Lord had backfired, Pilate was forced to find another means of dealing with this problem. He took Jesus back into the palace. He told his soldiers to og him (19:1). John tells us that when the soldiers beat our Lord, they clothed him in royal robes, put a crown of thorns on his head, and mockingly bowed down before him. Matthew 27:30 tells us that the soldiers also spit on the Lord Jesus and beat him over the head "again and again." The agony our Lord felt when they beat him with that rod was magnified because of the crown of thorns they had placed on his head. With every blow of the rod, it drove the thorns deeper into his skull. You cannot read this passage of Scripture without seeing the devil in all his fury lashing out at our Lord through these soldiers. This was not normal Roman procedure. Jesus had not been condemned. They had no right to og him. This was illegal cruelty at its worst.

I cannot read this passage without asking myself why

God would allow this to take place. This was no mere man they were beating. This was the Son of God, the Creator of the universe. Every ounce of energy needed to beat the Lord over the head with that rod came from God. Every breath they took to utter a blasphemous word against our Lord came from their Creator. How is it possible that mere men could so cruelly insult and beat the very Son of God without God the Father lashing out in revenge? In the days of Moses, when God descended on the mountain, even the smallest of animals who dared to step foot on it were to be destroyed. Here we have soldiers who tortured the Son of God without God's intervention. The only explanation for this is God's love for you and me. This is why God allowed these things to happen. He did it for us.

After this cruel beating, Pilate brought Jesus out again and presented him to the people. I believe that it was his hope that the people, on seeing how badly the Lord was beaten, would have been satisfied. When he presented Jesus to the crowd in his battered state, Pilate told them again that he found absolutely no fault in him.

There was no compassion from the crowd. Even this cruel punishment was not enough. They would not be happy until Jesus was dead. "Crucify! Crucify!" they shouted. "You take him and crucify him," Pilate responded, "As for me, I find no basis for a charge against him" (19:6). The Jews knew that they had no legal right to kill a man without the approval of the Roman authorities. They told Pilate that their law stated that he had to die because he claimed to be the Son of God.

When Pilate heard this, he was afraid (verse 8). We are not told why Pilate was afraid. Was he a religious man? Was he beginning to wonder who Jesus really was? There is no doubt that Pilate had heard what Jesus had been doing in Jerusalem. Stories abounded of the miracles he had performed. He took Jesus back into the palace for further questioning. "Where do you come from?" Pilate asked Jesus (verse 9). Jesus remained silent. "Don't you realize I have power either to free you or to crucify you?" questioned Pilate. Jesus reminded him, however, that he had no power but what was granted to him by his Father. Pilate was not in control of this situation. God held the reins. What an encouragement this is to us today. God is in control of even the worst of situations we face. The result of this conversation with Jesus was that Pilate sought even more to release him (verse 12).

Despite Pilate's attempts to free Jesus, the Jews continued to cry out for his crucifixion. They begin to accuse Pilate of political crimes. They told him that he could not be a friend of Caesar because Jesus claimed to be a king in opposition to Caesar. This placed Pilate in a very delicate situation. On the one hand, Pilate could do what he knew in his heart was right and release Jesus despite the cries of the crowd. On the other hand, he could pervert justice to please and quiet the crowd and save his reputation and title. What would be his decision?

Pilate brought Jesus out to the Jews for the last time. "Here is your king," he said. The crowd responded: "Take him away! Take him away! Crucify him!" (verse 15). "Shall I crucify your king?" asked Pilate. Was this a last feeble attempt to set Jesus free? "We have no king but Caesar," replied the crowd. Pilate knew the hypocrisy of this statement. The Jews resented the Roman presence in Israel.

Finally, Pilate handed Jesus over to the will of the Jews to crucify him. The Roman soldiers took Jesus and brought him to the Place of the Skull (Golgotha) where they nailed him to the cross with two criminals beside him. Pilate made a sign and fastened to the cross. The sign read: "JESUS OF NAZARETH, THE KING OF THE JEWS" (verse 19). The sign was written in Aramaic, Latin, and Greek, so that all could read it. When the Jewish leaders read this sign, they came to Pilate and asked him to change the wording. They wanted it to read: "This man claimed to be king of the Jews." Pilate refused their request. "What I have written, I have written," he told them (verse 22). Did he believe it himself? We do not know. Over the head of our Lord was the real reason he died. It was written for all to see. He died because he was the king of the Jews who had come to set them free from the bondage to sin.

You cannot read this passage of Scripture without being struck by Pilate and his attempts to deliver Jesus. There is no doubt that Pilate knew Jesus to be innocent. Why then did he crucify the Lord? He did so because of the pressure that the Jews put on him. He knew the truth but did not act on it. Knowing the truth is not enough.

For Consideration:

• Have you ever found yourself in a similar situation to Pilate? Were you called on to stand up for the Lord Jesus, but your desire to please the crowd stood in the way?

• What things stand in the way of you being a greater witness for the Lord Jesus today?

• What is the difference between knowing the truth and acting on that truth?

For Prayer:

• Take a moment to thank the Lord Jesus for what he endured for you on the cross of Calvary.

• Ask the Lord to give you boldness to take a stand for him.

• Pray for believers in positions of authority in our land. Ask God to give them boldness to stand firm for him and the principles of his Word.

50

That Scripture Might Be Fulfilled

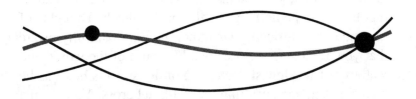

Read John 19:23–36

I t is never easy to understand suffering and death. What makes this passage even more difficult to understand is that this suffering and death took place in the life of the sinless Son of God. We saw in the last meditation that Pilate had declared Jesus to be innocent. He did not deserve to die. In this section, if there is one thing that the apostle John wants us to understand, it is that while our Lord did suffer, God was still in control. These events happened so that the Word of God, prophesied long before, would be fulfilled. John shares with us four incidents that took place at the cross that prove, beyond a shadow of a doubt, that God was working through this evil to fulfill his great overall plan.

Dividing Up Of Jesus' Clothes
The first of these events relates to what took place with the clothes of Jesus. It is important that we get the picture here. The soldiers had just taken our Lord and nailed him

to a cross. When they nailed him on the cross, they stripped him of his clothes. This added to his humiliation. It appears that there were four soldiers at the foot of the cross that day (verse 23). They took the clothes of our Lord and divided them among themselves. When they examined his coat and saw that it had value, they decided to cast lots for it.

Imagine for an instant that you are Mary, the mother of Jesus, or one of the disciples standing around the cross. As you look at what the soldiers have done to Jesus, you are horrified. You know that his trial was a false trial. You know that he had done nothing worthy of this death. Thoughts of injustice race through your mind. You are painfully aware that you are losing a close friend because of the hatred and jealousy of the Jewish leaders. You look at his body as he hangs, naked and suffering on that cruel cross. You see the marks of the whip and the blood, now drying on his esh. You see the bruises on his head where the Roman soldiers had repeatedly hit him with a rod. You are very aware of his pain. Your heart cries out: "God, why are you allowing this to happen?"

As these thoughts race through your mind, your attention is directed to a small group of soldiers at the foot of the cross. They seem oblivious to the agony of Christ on that cross. In his presence, they are dividing his clothes. To them this is an opportunity to enrich themselves. They have just cast lots, and one of them jumps up for joy because he has just won Jesus' coat. You immediately begin to think, "How can they be so insensitive? Are they not aware of the suffering that is taking place around them? How can they divide up Jesus' clothes right in front of the sufferers?"

The selfishness of the Roman soldiers was real. John was particularly sensitive to the pain of this incident. He was at the foot of the cross when these events were taking place. How does John help us deal with the pain of this event? He reminds us that this entire event had been predicted by the prophets many years prior to its happening. Psalm 22:18 tells us: "They divide my garments among them and cast lots for my clothing." The Psalmist prophesied of the insensitivity of the soldiers. Many years before these events, God foretold that these things would happen. God remained in control. This insensitivity was part of his overall plan. Though the enemy was very active, God was holding the reins. The soldiers only did what God predicted they would do.

Notice how the Lord met his friends in their pain. Jesus saw his mother and the disciple whom he loved (John), standing at the foot of the cross. He was particularly aware of the pain his mother was facing. Seeing her pain, Jesus told John to care for her as his own mother (verses 26–27). It is possible that Mary was a widow at this time. From that time on, John would care for Mary.

Wine Vinegar to Drink

The second event of importance in this passage relates to the soldiers who offered Jesus wine vinegar to drink. Our Lord became very thirsty because of his suffering on the cross. He cried out for something to drink. The soldiers dipped a sponge in wine vinegar and lifted it up to the Lord on a stock of hyssop. John reminds us that even this simple action had been predicted long before it had happened: "They put gall in my food and gave me vinegar for my thirst" (Psalms 69:21). When Jesus had taken the drink, he cried out: "It is finished," and he bowed his head and died (verse 30).

Breaking Of Jesus' Bones

The third prophecy accomplished at the cross relates to what took place after Jesus died. Because the Sabbath was drawing near, the Jews wanted the bodies taken down. To speed up the death of a criminal on the cross, the Romans would break their legs. The only way a crucified man could fill his lungs with air was to move his body using his legs. When his legs were broken, however, it would no longer be possible for him to breathe well. This hastened his death. The legs of the criminals on either side of our Lord were broken. When the soldiers came to Jesus, however, seeing that he was already dead, they chose not to break his legs.

John reminds us of how Exodus 12:46 commanded that the bones of the lambs sacrificed at Passover were not to be broken. The Passover lambs were the lambs killed for a special event when the Jews were in bondage in Egypt. The blood of these lambs, placed on the doorposts of their homes, protected the Jews from the angel of death who passed through Egypt to kill the firstborn son of every family. Jesus became our Passover Lamb. He was sacrificed so those who are covered by his blood are saved from the final judgment of God. It is significant, therefore, that the bones of the Lord Jesus were not broken.

Piercing Jesus' Side

Instead of breaking the bones of our Lord, the soldiers pierced his side. When his side was pierced, a mixture of water and blood gushed out of the wound (verse 34). Was this because of the severe beating our Lord had received? While we do not know where this blood came from, it is an indication of the damage that was done to his body by the soldiers who beat him and crucified him. His internal organs were seriously damaged. It is important to notice that Jesus died before those crucified at his side. This is also an indication of the intensity of suffering he had endured.

The prophet Zechariah clearly pointed to the piercing of Jesus' side in Zechariah 12:10: "And I will pour out on the house of David and the inhabitants of Jerusalem a spirit of grace and supplication. They will look on me, the one they have pierced, and they will mourn for him as one mourns for an only child, and grieve bitterly for him as one grieves for a firstborn son." Jesus is the perfect fulfillment of this prophecy given so long before he died.

The pain that our Lord endured had all been predicted down to the smallest detail. There was nothing that he endured which God did not know about and predict well in advance. Nothing takes God by surprise. Every trial in our lives has been calculated into his overall plan.

For Consideration:

- What encouragement do you take from the fact that all the suffering of Jesus was predicted long before it happened?

- Do you recall times when your suffering led to tremendous growth and victory in the end? Explain.

For Prayer:

- Thank the Lord that he knows all about your suffering and pain.

- Ask him to forgive you for the times you failed to understand his care for you in that suffering.

- Are you suffering right now? Commit yourself afresh into the hands of the Lord. Thank him that, in this particular suffering, he will care for you and work it all out for your good.

51

The Empty Tomb

Read John 19:38–20:31

J esus had been crucified. Joseph of Arimathea went to Pilate to ask for his body. Mark 15:43 tells us that Joseph was a member of the Jewish Council that had condemned Jesus to death. From Luke 23:50–51, however, we learn that he had not consented to their decision because he was an upright man. Pilate granted him permission to take the body of Jesus. Accompanied by Nicodemus, Joseph took down the body of Christ and prepared it for burial. Nicodemus, who accompanied Joseph, was the man who had come to Jesus in John 3 and later defended Jesus before his fellow Pharisees in John 7:50–51. When the body of Christ was prepared, Joseph and Nicodemus placed it in a tomb in a nearby garden (19:41–42).

Jesus did not remain in that tomb. He rose from the dead. Death could not hold him. We meet three individuals here in this passage. Each of them responded in a different way to the resurrection of their Lord.

Mary Magdalene

On the first day of the week, very early in the morning, Mary Magdalene went to the grave site (20:1). Obviously, her soul was troubled. She wanted to see where they had put her Lord. Beyond these natural reasons, however, God himself was directing her to the tomb. Unknown to her at the time, God had called her to announce the resurrection of Christ.

As she approached the tomb, she noticed that the stone was rolled away. Though Jesus had told his followers that he would rise from the dead, Mary had not understood. Why would that stone be rolled away? To Mary the only explanation was that the Jews had stolen Christ's body.

This discovery troubled Mary. She rushed back with the news that they had taken the body of Christ. She had made a very logical conclusion based on what she had seen, but she was wrong. Even today there are many, like Mary, who seek to explain away the miraculous resurrection of our Lord. Theories abound as to why the tomb was empty. Satan surely realized that if he could explain away the resurrection of Christ, the result would be a Christianity with no hope. If Christ is still dead, then our faith is vain (1 Corinthians 15:17).

The exciting thing about this story of Mary Magdalene is that God did not leave her in her despair. Mary returned to the tomb with some of the disciples. We will look at their responses later. When these disciples left the empty tomb, Mary remained and wept. Something caused her to look inside. There inside the tomb she saw two angels. "Woman, why are you crying?" they asked Mary (verse 13). "They have taken my Lord away," was her response. Having said this, Mary became aware of another presence near her. She turned around and saw Jesus, but she did not recognize him. She thought he was the gardener. "Sir, if you carried him away, tell me where you have put him, and I will get him," she said (verse 15). Her desire was that the Lord Jesus have a proper burial. Her love for him was such that she could not bear the thought of his body being carelessly thrown into an unmarked grave.

Seeing her anguish, Jesus called out her name. "Mary," he said. There was something about that voice. There was no voice like it. She looked up and recognized Jesus at once. She threw her arms around him. She had been wrong. Jesus was alive. When she saw him, every ounce of doubt was removed.

Mary was brought from despair to hope through her personal encounter with the risen Lord. Our doubting world needs this personal encounter with Jesus. We know him to be alive because we too, like Mary, have met him. He called out my name too, and I recognized his voice. We now have hope. Our faith is not in vain. Jesus is alive. We know this because we have met him personally.

Jesus told Mary that she was not to keep this news to herself. She was to go and tell his disciples. That command has not changed. If you know Jesus to be alive today, you too are to go and tell the good news to others.

Peter and the Unnamed Disciple

When Mary Magdalene had first gone to the disciples to tell them that someone had removed the body of the Lord from the tomb, two of them had immediately left for the tomb (20:1–3). Peter was one of those disciples. The other is unnamed. While the unnamed disciple arrived first, he waited for Peter's arrival before entering the tomb. When Peter entered, he saw the grave clothes, but Jesus was not there. Verse 8 tells us that when Peter saw the clothes, he believed. Peter believed that the Lord had risen and was alive.

Peter's response was very different from Mary's. Though

he had not yet seen the Lord Jesus, he believed that he had risen. What caused him to believe? The passage tells us that they still did not understand from Scripture that Jesus was to rise from the dead (verse 9). Jesus had often taught them that he would rise from the dead. Though Peter did not understand how all these things fit into the context of the Scriptures, he still believed that what he was seeing was a fulfillment of prophecy. He did not understand, but he believed. Mary had a very dramatic encounter with the Lord Jesus himself. All Peter had was the words that Jesus spoke when he was with them.

Not everyone has a dramatic encounter with the Lord as Mary did. For some of us, all we will have is the words that Jesus spoke as recorded for us in the Scriptures. Some come to faith in Christ through mystical and dramatic experiences as Mary had. Others come to him by a simple and quiet examination of the facts.

Thomas

Jesus appeared to his disciples soon after his resurrection (verse19). The disciples were gathered behind locked doors when Jesus appeared to them. Why the doors were locked, we are not told. Having killed the Lord Jesus, the Jews would not have been happy to leave his disciples alone. The disciples would have been subject to attack and persecution from the Jews who had killed their Lord.

When Jesus appeared to his disciples that day, he commissioned them to go and tell others the good news (verse 21). Although at this time they were afraid for their lives, the time was coming when they would unlock those doors and boldly proclaim the truth about Christ. In order for this to happen, they would need the presence and enabling of the Holy Spirit. Jesus' death had paved the way for them to be forgiven and indwelled by the Holy Spirit. In his strength, they would move out with the message of the gospel. As they moved out in the power of the Holy Spirit, they would have the power of the forgiveness of sin at their disposal (verse 23). This is not to say that they were able to forgive sin themselves. The Holy Spirit who indwelled them would use them to convict the world of sin. As they went in Jesus' name and in the power of his Spirit with the message of forgiveness through Christ, men and women would be forgiven of their sin and come to new life. Those who rejected their message and the offer they brought would be condemned. Those who received their message would experience the wonderful forgiveness of God.

Thomas was not with the disciples that day. When he returned, the disciples told him that they had seen the Lord. John does not tell us how many disciples were present in the room that day. Thomas, in spite of the many witnesses who surrounded him, would not believe. "Unless I see the nail marks in his hands and put my finger where the nails were, and put my hand into his side, I will not believe it," he said (verse 25).

A week later, the Lord returned to the disciples. This time Thomas was with them. Jesus spoke to Thomas: "Put your finger here; see my hands. Reach out your hand and put it into my side. Stop doubting and believe" (verse 27). It was only when Thomas met the Lord for himself that he truly believed. "My Lord and my God," he cried. There would be no doubting now for Thomas.

There are many people like Thomas today. These individuals surround themselves with Christians but still have many doubts. The Lord can reveal himself to these individuals so that they never doubt again.

The apostle John reminds us in verse 30 that while there are many more miracles that Jesus did, John specifically chose these miracles so that those who read this Gospel would believe in the Lord Jesus and have eternal life. Thomas needed to put his hands in Jesus' side to believe.

John realized that there would be many people, like Thomas, who would not believe unless they saw the miracle of the risen Lord before them. John filled his book with stories of Jesus' miracles. All who will open their eyes can see evidence in these miracles that "Jesus is the Christ, the Son of God" (verse 31).

The evidence is before us as well. Will we be like Mary and explain it away? Will we be like Thomas and surround ourselves with believers but be full of doubt? Will we be like the disciple who entered the tomb and, seeing the evidence, believed? Everyone must make a choice. Praise God that each of these individuals eventually came to believe in Christ. The circumstances may be different. What is important is not how we come to believe but that we eventually do come to believe in Christ, and "by believing . . . have life in his name" (verse 31).

For Consideration:

- How did you come to believe in the Lord Jesus? What was it that convinced you of the reality of his claims?

- Notice how the Lord meets each of the individuals in this passage in a different way. Consider how the Lord has revealed himself to you, your friends, and loved ones. What does this teach us about God?

For Prayer:

- Do you know of someone who questions the reality of the claims of Jesus? Take a moment to pray that the Lord would reveal himself to this person in a way that leaves no doubt.

- Thank the Lord that, despite our lack of faith, he reveals himself to us anyway.

- Thank him that he meets us as individuals, each with our different needs and shortcomings.

52

God's Way and Man's Way

Read John 21:1–14

Jesus no longer ministered with his disciples. He only met with them occasionally. In Jesus' absence, the disciples were quite confused about what they were to do with their lives. On this occasion, Peter and six other disciples decided to go fishing. They got into a boat and fished all night without catching anything. In the early hours of the morning, they heard a voice calling out to them: "Friends, haven't you any fish?" "No," they replied (verse 5). "Throw your net on the right side of the boat and you will find some," came the response (verse 6). This advice made no sense. There was something about that voice, however, that made them listen. They drew up their net and put them back into the water on the right side of the boat. Immediately their net was full of fish, too numerous to even haul into the boat.

These disciples knew all the tricks of the fishing trade. They had no need of anyone to tell them how to fish. They had carefully chosen the location to anchor their boat. They had set out their net with the skill of experienced anglers. They did what any good angler would do, but they had not caught any fish.

Some of the greatest lessons we need to learn in our Christian life are to be able to wait on the Lord, discern his voice, and obey it. All too often, we run ahead of the Lord. We are confident in our abilities to handle matters. Like the disciples, we know all the tricks of the trade. We feel like we do not need anyone to tell us what to do. We forge ahead with our projects and programs, without taking time to seek the Lord. We sit in our boat with our nets dangling over the side but catch nothing. Our schedules are full, but our lives are unfruitful.

What a difference it makes, however, when we learn to wait on the Lord and follow his leading. Our nets over ow with blessing. This does not mean that we cast aside our experience, education, and talents. Notice here in this story that the Lord used the disciples' skills as fishermen. Their skills were stretched to the maximum as they dealt with the multitude of fish the Lord put in their net.

In the same way, the Lord wants to use your gifts, education, and personality. He wants to stretch these abilities to the maximum. As the Master of the harvest, he sends his workers out to do what he has equipped them to do. He asks one to wait and another to act immediately. He knows exactly what he is doing. Sometimes, however, we take matters into our own hands. We do not listen to the Master of the harvest. We do things in our own way. The result is mass confusion on the harvest field. Each worker seems to be working independently. How much farther ahead we would be if only we were willing to let him direct us.

John saw the significance of this miracle. He immediately recognized that it was the Lord speaking to them from the shore. When Peter heard this, he left the net, jumped into the water, and swam to shore. He left the other disciples to fight with the fish. The Bible tells us that they caught 153 large fish that day (verse 11). What surprised them even more was the fact that though the net had been stretched beyond its limit, it had not torn. That net did more than it was physically capable of doing. In the same way, God provides us with the strength and ability necessary to do what he calls us to do. You may, like this net, be stretched beyond your human abilities, but God will not allow you to be broken. His strength and enabling will match your trial.

This passage teaches us the importance of hearing the voice of the Lord. It reminds us of how often we have done things in our own way and in our own strength. It promises great blessings for those who will listen to the voice of him who calls out from the shore. It reminds us that the Lord is in the business of using our strengths and talents to accomplish his great overall plan. He will stretch us beyond our abilities but will always provide us with the strength necessary for the task.

For Consideration:

• Are you hearing the voice of the Lord? What is the difference between doing things in your own human strength and waiting on the Lord to use you to do things in his strength?

• Take a moment to examine where you are today. Are you confident that you are in the will and purpose of the Lord?

• How much of what you do is based on your own wisdom and talents, and how much is based on truly seeking God and his will?

• How does God communicate his will to us today?

For Prayer:

- Ask God to forgive you for the times you have not sought his will and his plans.

- Ask the Lord to help you to hear, understand, and follow his leading each day.

- Take a moment to pray for your spiritual leaders. Ask God to teach them to listen to his voice and not to depend on their own strength and wisdom.

53

Unlikely Candidates

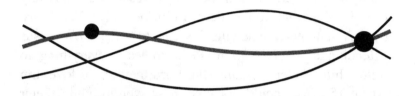

Read John 21:15–25

After a very successful catch, the disciples were now bringing their boat to shore. Jesus had told them to cast their net on the right side of the boat. When they had obeyed, their net filled with fish. Understanding that it was Jesus on the shore, Peter had jumped out of the boat and hurried to meet him. He had left the other disciples to haul in their great catch of fish.

After a breakfast of bread and fish, the Lord Jesus turned his attention to Peter. "Simon son of John, do you truly love me more than these?" There is some confusion here as to what Jesus meant by this statement. Is Jesus asking Peter if he loved him more than the other disciples did? Peter did have a tendency to compare himself to others. Listen to what he had once told Jesus: "Even if all fall away on account of you, I never will" (Matthew 26:33). Peter had set himself above the other disciples in this passage. Was Jesus asking Peter to re-examine his statement now that he had denied him three times? How might Peter feel about that statement now that he had failed miserably?

It may also be possible that the Lord was asking Peter if he loved him more than he loved his former occupation as a fisherman. Scattered around them was their fishing equipment. Was Jesus asking Peter if he was willing to leave his fishing to follow him? Maybe this took Peter back about three years to the day that Jesus called him to leave his fishing nets and follow him. Peter had recently denied the Lord. Maybe Peter was wondering if Jesus could possibly use him now that he had denied him publicly. Was Jesus, by this statement, renewing his call to Peter? Was Jesus extending a second call to Peter to leave everything to follow him? Peter reassured the Lord that he did love him (verse 15). We should not take these words lightly. Peter had already confidently spoken these words to the Lord, but he had since fallen. Jesus gave him an opportunity here to renew his commitment to him. Peter did so, but this time he did so with the understanding that he could fall.

Hearing Peter's response, Jesus told him to feed his lambs. The test of Peter's love for his Lord would be his love for those who belonged to him. What Jesus was telling Peter that day was that if Peter loved him, he would care for the Lord's children. This would not be easy for Peter. Peter was more of a leader and visionary than a pastor. Just that morning when he recognized that it was the Lord on the shore, he had left his fellow disciples behind to fend for themselves. If Peter were the pastoral type, he would have remained with the others to help them with their burden.

Peter had a real tendency to do things in his own way. He was the self-proclaimed spokesman for the rest of the disciples. He had many rough edges in his spiritual life. It was not easy for him to hold his tongue. He often acted without thinking. Sometimes he saw himself as being better than others. At times he became jealous. (See verse 21–23.)

He had a tremendous confidence in himself and in his way of doing things. He would jump into things without thinking about others. Is this the type of person you would want for a pastor? It would not be easy for this man to tend to the needs of the sheep. There was much humbling that needed to take place.

Three times, Jesus asked Peter if he loved him. Three times, Peter told the Lord that he did. Three times, Jesus reminded him that he was to care for his sheep. Did Jesus ask Peter to reconfirm his love to him three times because he had denied him three times? What is important for us to note here is that while Peter had denied the Lord, he was not abandoned by God. He had fallen   at on his face. He had a lot to learn, but Jesus was giving him a second chance.

Sometimes the Lord uses the most unlikely people. It would be so easy for us to condemn Peter with all his personality faults, but God had chosen him and would not let him go. This teaches us not to be so judgmental regarding our spiritual leadership. They may not be perfect, but they are called of God. We must accept them as God's instruments to accomplish his purposes.

Jesus reminded Peter that this responsibility he was giving to him would not be easy. "When you were younger you dressed yourself and went where you wanted; but when you are old you will stretch out your hands, and someone else will dress you and lead you where you do not want to go" (verse 18). Peter would discover that he no longer had control over his life. Others would decide what he would do and where he would go. Again, we need to be reminded of how difficult that would be for Peter. Peter liked to do things in his own way. The day was coming when all that would change. God had not finished the work he was doing in Peter's life. In the coming years, Peter would be molded by the circumstances that God sent his way. God would shape him into a vessel of honor. He would strip him of his control over his own circumstances and shape him through this.

God knows what needs to happen in each of our lives. In the case of the apostle Paul, God left him with a physical infirmity to humble him (2 Corinthians 12:8–10). Here in Peter's case, God would strip him of his self-confidence by the foreordained circumstances he would face in life. The problems and difficulties that come our way are God's means of shaping us into the people he wants us to be.

Notice Peter's response to the Lord's prophetic word. Peter looked at John, and asked: "What about him?" (verse 21). Why was Peter so concerned about John? Did he again feel compelled to compare himself to the other disciples? Was he speaking out of jealousy? Jesus had predicted that Peter's future would be difficult. He would be forced to do things he did not want to do. The passage tells us that Jesus had said these things to indicate what sort of death Peter would suffer. Peter had just been reminded of his shortcomings. Deep inside, Peter had to know what would happen to John. John was the disciple whom Jesus loved. Would his life be any easier than Peter's?

Jesus did not give Peter the satisfaction of an answer: "If I want him to remain alive until I return, what is that to you? You must follow me," responded Jesus (verse 22). Jesus was telling Peter here that it did not matter what he did with John. God's purpose for John was different from his purpose for Peter.

Many of us, like Peter, have a tendency to measure our spirituality and success in ministry by comparing ourselves to others. God's purpose for us is not his purpose for another. We must learn to be content to do what the Lord calls us to do.

Because of what Jesus said that day about John, news spread that John would not die. John reminds us, however, that this was not what Jesus meant. He was simply using this as an example for the purpose of challenging Peter with his proud attitude.

John also reminds us that there were many other things that Jesus did that are not recorded (verse 25). What he has recorded for us is but a sample of the great works of our Lord. All these miracles, however, were chosen by John to help us understand who Jesus is, so that we might come to faith in him.

As I close the final chapter of this book, I want to remind you that the Lord sometimes chooses the most unlikely people. Here before us in this passage is a man by the name of Peter. He was far from perfect. He had failed his Lord on many occasions. He had many personal obstacles to overcome. God put his hand on him, however, and chose to work through him. Maybe you are like Peter today. Your past is not very glorious. You have many personal and spiritual obstacles to overcome in your walk with the Lord. Isn't it good to know that the Lord is still willing to use you? Let him take you and shape you as he did with Peter? Yield your life to him. Commit yourself to seeking him and allowing his Word to shape you. He will use you beyond your greatest expectations.

For Consideration:

• What are some of the "rough edges" in your life?

• The proof of Peter's love for the Lord would be seen in his devotion to the "flock." What is the proof of your love for the Lord?

• Have you ever, like Peter, failed in your relationship with the Lord? What does this passage teach you about being restored?

- What is the connection here between loving God and loving his children?

For Prayer:

- Thank the Lord that he is willing to use you as you are.

- Ask the Lord to particularly deal with those "rough edges" in your spiritual life.

- Ask the Lord to forgive you for the times you have failed him and those you love.

Light To My Path
Devotional Commentary Series

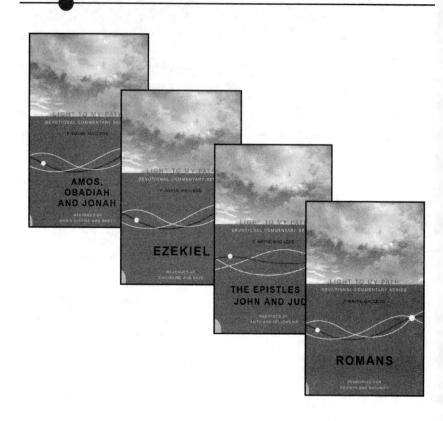

Now Available

Old Testament

- Ezra, Nehemiah, and Esther
- Ezekiel
- Amos, Obadiah, and Jonah
- Micah, Nahum, Habakkuk, and Zephaniah

New Testament

- John
- Acts
- Romans
- The Epistles of John and Jude

A new commentary series
for every day devotional use.

"I am impressed by what I have read from this set of commentaries. I have found them to be concise, insightful, inspiring, practical and, above all, true to Scripture. Many will find them to be excellent resources."

Randy Alcorn
director of Eternal Perspective Ministries,
Author of *The Grace & Truth Paradox*
and *Money, Possessions & Eternity*

Watch for more in the series
Spring 2005

Old Testament
- Israel
- Haggai, Zachariah and Malachi

New Testament
- Philippians and Colossians
- James and 1&2 Peter

Other books available from
Authentic Media . . .

Authentic
MEDIA

PO Box 1047
129 Mobilization Drive
Waynesboro, GA 30830

706-554-1594
1-8MORE-BOOKS
ordersusa@stl.org

Power of Generosity
How to Transform Yourself and Your World

David Toycen

An intimate journey down the road of giving, *The Power of Generosity* will strike a chord with all who want to fulfill a vital part of their humanity–the need to give.

Dave Toycen, President and CEO of World Vision Canada, believes generosity can save lives—both the benefactor's and the recipient's. The act of giving without an ulterior motive inherently nurtures a need human's have for significance. During three decades of traveling to the poorest and most desperate countries, Dave has seen and met individuals who have been freed by acts of generosity.

What is generosity? What motivates a person toward benevolence? *The Power of Generosity* is a practical guide to developing a spirit of generosity, providing thoughtful answers and encouragement for all those looking for ways to be more giving in their lives.

1-932805-10-9   192 Pages

Cat and Dog Theology
Rethinking Our Relationship With Our Master

Bob Sjogren & Dr. Gerald Robison

There is a joke about cats and dogs that conveys their differences perfectly.

> A dog says, "You pet me, you feed me, you shelter me, you love me, you must be God."
>
> A cat says, "You pet me, you feed me, you shelter me, you love me, I must be God."

These God-given traits of cats ("You exist to serve me") and dogs ("I exist to serve you") are often similar to the theological attitudes we have in our view of God and our relationship to Him. Using the differences between cats and dogs in a light-handed manner, the authors compel us to challenge our thinking in deep and profound ways. As you are drawn toward God and the desire to reflect His glory in your life, you will worship, view missions, and pray in a whole new way. This life-changing book will give you a new perspective and vision for God as you delight in the God who delights in you.

1-884543-17-0   206 Pages

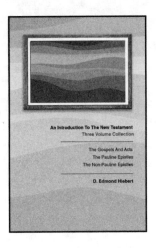

An Introduction To The New Testament
Three Volume Collection

D. Edmond Hiebert

Though not a commentary, the Introduction to the New Testament presents each book's message along with a discussion of such questions as authorship, composition, historical circumstances of their writing, issues of criticism and provides helpful, general information on their content and nature. The bibliographies and annotated book list are extremely helpful for pastors, teachers, and laymen as an excellent invitation to further careful exploration.

This book will be prized by all who have a desire to delve deeply into the New Testament writings.

Volume 1: The Gospels And Acts
Volume 2: The Pauline Epistles
Volume 3: The Non-Pauline Epistles and Revelation

1-884543-74-X   976 Pages